Rapid Results!

Robert H. Schaffer

Ronald N. Ashkenas

and Associates

Rapid Results!

How 100-Day Projects Build the Capacity for Large-Scale Change

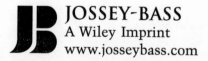

JOSSEY-BASS
A Wiley Imprint
www.josseybass.com

Published by Jossey-Bass
A Wiley Imprint
989 Market Street, San Francisco, CA 94103-1741   www.josseybass.com

Readers should be aware that Internet Web sites offered as citations and/or sources for further
information may have changed or disappeared between the time this was written and when it
is read.

Jossey-Bass books and products are available through most bookstores. To contact Jossey-Bass
directly call our Customer Care Department within the U.S. at 800-956-7739, outside the
U.S. at 317-572-3986, or fax 317-572-4002.

Jossey-Bass also publishes its books in a variety of electronic formats. Some content that
appears in print may not be available in electronic books.

Library of Congress Cataloging-in-Publication Data

Schaffer, Robert H.
    Rapid results! : how 100-day projects build the capacity for large-scale change /
Robert H. Schaffer, Ronald N. Ashkenas and Associates —1st ed.
        p. cm.
    Includes bibliographical references and index.
    ISBN-13 978-0-7879-7734-4 (alk. paper)
    ISBN-10 0-7879-7734-9 (alk. paper)
    1. Organizational change—Management. 2. Organizational effectiveness.
I. Ashkenas, Ronald N. II. Title.
HD58.8.S298 2005
658.1'6—dc22   2005004546

Printed in the United States of America
FIRST EDITION
HB Printing   10 9 8 7 6 5 4 3 2

Contents

Part Four: Conclusion

Preface

This book is addressed to leaders who are impatient with the pace of progress in their organizations. These leaders know they must achieve more—faster. They are unwilling to rationalize that everything will work out OK; instead they are determined to get their organizations performing at a much higher level, executing large-scale changes much more rapidly. If you are one of these leaders, you undoubtedly have been making substantial investments on many fronts—new information systems and automation, R&D, new product development. You may have acquired companies. You have invested energy in creating new views of the business. And you have made many other strategic investments. Yet despite all the progress, you are uneasy that your organization's pace may not be fast enough to ensure success in the dynamic world of the twenty-first century.

The book describes how the use of rapid results projects can, in a short time, multiply your power to make large-scale changes succeed. These are projects that produce results very quickly and that also introduce new work patterns and enable participants to learn all sorts of lessons about managing change. No matter what kind of shift your organization may need, tens or hundreds of successful rapid-cycle projects occurring simultaneously can deliver tangible results—while at the same time developing the basic capability and confidence to support the whole process.

To understand the approach and to benefit from it, however, you have to take a deep breath and liberate yourself from the layers of management beliefs about what you must do if you want to make major shifts in performance or direction.

Preparations Now—Results Some Day

Virtually everyone who advises managers on how to accelerate the pace of change adheres to the same basic formula: if you want to be rewarded with better performance or more rapid change, you must first lay down the foundations that will enable the changes to take place—later. Install the right IT systems. Recruit better people. Train the people you have. Reorganize. Create the right culture. Develop more innovative products. Develop the right long-term strategies. And straighten out everything else that needs to be straightened out. Once you've done it all, results will surely follow. But be prepared to spend lots of time and lots of resources preparing and gearing up. Don't dare look for gains tomorrow—or even the next day.

Yes, all the experts agree: seeking short-term rewards is a prime sin of management. And managers have been trained to feel slightly ashamed of themselves when they try to attain some immediate benefit. The spirit is captured beautifully in this Request for Proposals our firm received from a potential client: "While the intent [of the project] is to find opportunities to deliver savings next year or even earlier. . . . *Short-term gains that could undermine the long-term organizational capability will not be acceptable*" (italics added).

Watch out, this management is saying! We know that if you focus on short-term results they will necessitate moves that are essentially unhealthy. You could be advancing tactical gains at the expense of strategic gains. You could be wasting resources on the wrong efforts. You could be investing in the wrong products or the wrong services. You might be centralizing when you should be decentralizing.

Much better to wait till all the data is assembled, the plans are developed, the systems all speak to each other, the organization is beefed up, and all the other needed improvements are carried out.

Logical! Irrefutable!

Yes, and completely wrong.

Short-Term Results—Energizer for More

Our evidence suggests that the most powerful driver of better performance is better performance itself. That is, if you want to help an organization develop its ability to perform better you can do nothing more effective than help it to experience a tangible success on some of the dimensions it is trying to strengthen.

The process has succeeded in hundreds of organizations. The secret is to turn the "begin-with-preparations-and-wait-patiently-for-results" paradigm upside down and begin at once with results. That means that if you want to enter a completely new market, you start not by doing a market analysis but by making a test probe into that market, right away. If you want to grow faster, you begin not with a study to analyze growth opportunities but by accelerating the growth of one product, or with one customer—now, right away—and do it in a way that strengthens your capacity for larger-scale advance.

The success of this methodology exposes as fiction one of the few universally accepted "truths" of organization management—the notion that a short-term focus is always bad. That old saw is the legacy of too many panicky short-term moves that have damaged companies—like cutting R&D or eliminating customer services. We have discovered that short-term thrusts can be powerfully beneficial if they are executed intelligently and if they are designed as stepping-stones toward major strategic gains. Short-term thrusts are bad only when stupidly conceived or stupidly executed.

This book, reflecting decades of successful experience, extols and glorifies short-term successes—not as an alternative to a long-term strategic perspective but as a vital, though frequently missing, element of corporate progress.

Corporate Improvement Processes— Like Organ Transplants

Everyone knows that in organ transplantation the health of the replacement organ and the skill of the surgeon doing the operation mean nothing unless steps are taken to ensure that the introduced organ will work compatibly with the hundreds of other physical, chemical, and biological systems in the receiving body. Without this compatibility the transplant will fail.

This concept applies equally to the introduction of large-scale organization change and improvement. When a new improvement effort—a new business strategy, a major cost improvement program, or a new technology—is transplanted into the organization, its success depends on the capacity of the organization to establish the hundreds or thousands of new work patterns and communications flows necessary to absorb the new transplant.

Unfortunately, improvement efforts are typically inserted into the body of organizations with little or no consideration for compatibility. If the transplant is seen as a key to improvement, it is installed even though the organization may contain dozens of processes that will not work well with it or that may outright reject it. This top-down, big-fix approach to implanting major change frequently fails because of the lack of absorption capability throughout the organization.

Rapid-cycle projects reverse the process: they achieve quick results in a way that helps participants learn how to mesh new approaches into the broader organization patterns. And they quickly develop the organization's capacity to absorb all sorts of transplants without generating chaos. They help to eliminate the long lag times and deadly inertia that often impede urgently needed progress. And they engage people in the learning and discovery needed to make change stick. That's how they open the pathway to larger and more far-reaching changes.

Multiple Benefits That Are Constantly Expanding

By expanding implementation capability at every level, rapid results projects enable the organization to carry out large-scale change quickly and effectively. They can also make a number of other vital contributions:

- They provide a method for translating large-scale conceptual and strategic visions into workable actions. Companies often create bold and ambitious strategic visions, but achieving them seems too complex and risky. So action is delayed. The rapid results approach allows companies to move forward with action and get some benefits quickly in a low-risk fashion no matter how complex the overall goals being pursued.

- They develop powerful leadership skills by providing experience in new modes of achieving results and new modes of collaboration.

- They engage large numbers of people—not just a few experts—in working on improvement and innovation.

- They encourage the testing of new forms of partnership with customers and suppliers, along with new kinds of collaboration across organization boundaries.

As increasing numbers of these rapid-cycle projects are carried out, a go-for-it feeling begins to develop throughout the organization. Out of big, amorphous goals, short-term targets are set. Team accountabilities are specified. Work plans are developed. As projects succeed, participants absorb the learning and move on to more ambitious and sophisticated undertakings. And as implementation capability expands, so does the organization's capacity to master its strategic direction. In other words, the culture of the enterprise begins to shift—even though the focus is on tangible results and not on culture change.

Some people who are not familiar with the approach have reacted to the description of rapid-cycle projects by saying, "Oh yes, you pluck the low-hanging fruit"—implying that the approach is based on exploiting things that are easy to do. But while we see nothing wrong with accomplishing easy goals, the rapid results process helps people to carve off achievable steps from difficult goals as a step toward achieving those goals. The book describes how that occurs—how, for example, Avery Dennison used the approach to achieve $50 million of new sales within a year and radically modified its growth strategies as a result. Georgia-Pacific achieved many hundreds of millions of dollars of measurable annual improvement, plus carrying out a number of strategic shifts. One oil company reduced operating costs by $250 million, and an insurance company captured $60 million in improvements using the approach.[1]

No, rapid results projects go way beyond low-hanging fruit.

As Timely as Timely Can Be

We believe that achieving more rapid results and learning from those successes is one of the most critical challenges facing leaders of organizations today. Throughout the industrialized world, many of the familiar pathways to success from the 1980s and 1990s seem unworkable in the twenty-first century. Large numbers of companies throughout the world are struggling. Many more senior managers are engaging in fraud and deception in a desperate effort to succeed. Large numbers of employees and managers at all levels are anxious about their futures. Governments seem less able to stimulate their economies or develop the infrastructure necessary to support economic growth.

Paradoxically, every day that passes sees the power and speed of information technology rapidly expanding. Yet human capabilities remain virtually unchanged. Any approach to change needs to help human organizations break free of human limitations and must be keyed to the speed and excitement of the Internet age. This means change methods that have human scale with Internet speed.

Strongly as we advocate rapid-cycle successes as critical to achieving this accelerated pace, we do not suggest that they take the place of the other key elements—strategy, technology, human resource management. What the rapid-cycle projects do is to help create an environment where all the elements can be brought into play effectively and with mutual reinforcement. It is a mode of change that begins with a result—a result that can be achieved in weeks or months at the most. Each project is used to test innovations and build the capability of individuals and the organization as a whole. And it introduces a sense of speed.

A rapid-cycle success, in short, is an adrenaline-charged change—fast-moving, exciting, energizing, and ultimately transforming—the perfect complement to the age of speed.

A Powerful and Well-Tested Methodology

Unlike most of the literature about change management, this book describes methodologies that have been validated and revalidated in the crucible of real organization change over many years. The authors have devoted most of their professional lives to developing these approaches and using them to help organizations of every size and description to improve performance and speed the pace of change. During the time that the process has taken shape in hundreds of applications, the authors have constantly written about the ideas as they were evolving—in five earlier books and more than 150 articles.[2] *Rapid Results!* brings it all together. It captures the essential lessons from the decades of dedicated effort.

The book will show you that you *can* have your cake and eat it too. It describes how you can attain rapid results with quick paybacks and do it in a way that will develop your fundamental capacity to achieve the longest-term and most far-reaching gains. Yes, the pursuit of immediate gratification, properly conducted, can open the door to long-term success.

How the Book Was Written

This book is a shared undertaking by members of Robert H. Schaffer & Associates. Robert Schaffer and Ronald Ashkenas took the lead in conceiving the book and designing its structure. The associates with the greatest expertise in each topic area, including Schaffer and Ashkenas, were the main authors of the appropriate chapters. These include Suzanne C. Francis, Nadim F. Matta, Matthew K. McCreight, Keith E. Michaelson, Robert A. Neiman, and Harvey A. Thomson. Schaffer did the major share of working with these colleagues to ensure that you will be reading a single book—not a collection of writings—and Ashkenas provided overall editorial guidance.

Many of the case illustrations in the book involved projects in which RHS&A participated as consultants. We have not described our role (or that of other consultants) in the cases because this book emphasizes the method, not the consulting help. Almost all the case illustrations are, with the subject's consent, identified. We have maintained anonymity where an organization is being criticized unless the information has already been published.

What You'll Find Ahead

Part One, the first three chapters, lays out the basic concepts about rapid-cycle projects—what they are, how they differ from other improvement processes, and why they possess unique power to stimulate success.

Then Part Two describes how rapid results projects create a strong foundation for carrying out major changes in direction and large-scale advances in operational performance. We show how, by developing the many dimensions of implementation capability in an organization, rapid results projects multiply the return from available resources while expanding overall change capability.

The chapters in Part Three describe how to use the expanded (and continuously expanding) capability that is the product of rapid results projects in implementing major strategic or operational shifts. With examples from both companies and countries, we show how to attack large-scale changes by building on a foundation of confidence and learning generated by many rapid-cycle projects.

And finally, Chapter Twelve describes how senior leaders of organizations, with the help of their staff and consulting resources, can shift their own personal work strategies to fully exploit the opportunities for major return outlined in the book.

July 2005　　　　　　　　　　　　　　　ROBERT H. SCHAFFER
Stamford, Connecticut　　　　　　　　　RONALD N. ASHKENAS

Rapid Results!

Part One

IMPLEMENTATION CAPABILITY

Strengthening the Weakest Link

Part One sheds a spotlight on the importance of implementation capacity—the ability to make the hundreds or thousands of changes at the grassroots level that must occur for large-scale change to succeed. It describes the power of projects that achieve rapid results and that simultaneously build the capacity of the organization to achieve even more results.

It describes why these projects not only energize and stimulate people at every level but also develop the organization's fundamental implementation capacity.

1

A THOUSAND CURES

Which One Is Right?

Like a broken record, business authors, journalists, government leaders, and economists continue to warn that the pace of change is accelerating, and that managers need to move faster, get ahead of the curve, be more proactive, reduce cycle times, speed up production. Speed is everything. Speed is winning. Speed is surviving.

The messages are unrelenting, but they are off-target: the leaders of our corporations and other institutions don't need this advice. They are acutely aware of the forces reshaping the environment in which they operate. They see what has been happening to the U.S. automobile industry in the forty years since it began responding to the competition from fuel-efficient, high-quality cars from Japan—and then from Europe. They saw what happened to IBM when the personal computer changed the information management model. They see globalization sweeping hundreds of thousands of jobs from one country to another. They see technology rapidly obsolescing the mainstays of traditional economies, like telephony. They see digital imaging driving companies like Kodak and Polaroid into life-and-death struggles. They watch awestruck as Wal-Mart moves across the landscape leveling virtually everything in its way.

No, those who are leading major organizations today don't need to be told to wake up to the issue of change. They want to know what they can do about accelerating change. How can they respond to these challenges in ways that will ensure success?

The good news for managers who want more insight into how they can master major change is that tons of advice on that subject have been published in the past twenty years. But the bad news is that consulting the most popular parts of that literature will yield not an answer but a thousand answers. Moreover, the answers generally consist of fragmented elements of change ideas rather than comprehensive, tested change strategies.

Worse, most of the formulas consist of large-scale, go-for-broke change efforts. These titanic programs, mainly consultant-inspired and installed at astronomical fees, carry a high risk of disappointment.

Rapid Results is different. It presents a comprehensive change strategy, but it begins in ways that pay their way almost at once, that require no major investment, and that are very low risk. This chapter introduces the concept and shows how it can serve as the fundamental building block of large-scale change.

Overlooked Opportunity

In our years of work with hundreds of organizations all over the world, we have encountered virtually none where it was not possible to generate fresh, reinforcing, improved results within a very short time—several months at most. And by *results* we mean real, tangible, bottom-line results: increased sales. Reduced turnaround time. Increased inventory turns. New products marketed more rapidly. Welfare services provided more effectively.

This has been true of large, well-known corporations like General Electric, Avery Dennison, Georgia-Pacific, Siemens AG, GlaxoSmithKline, Citigroup, Motorola, and Zurich Financial Services, as we detail later in the book. It has been true of many smaller companies. It has been true of hospitals and schools. It has been true of city and state governments. It has been true of agricultural and health organizations and government agencies in developing countries.

Not only is it fairly straightforward to generate results quickly, such projects can serve as the foundation and backbone of large-scale, sustained change and improvement. In fact, because of their capacity not only to yield immediate payback but also to lay the foundation for large-scale change, we have found that such rapid results projects are the best way to launch any major change or improvement effort. What is most surprising about this phenomenon is how few managers or consultants use this powerful approach and how few organization researchers have opened their eyes to the possibilities.

The Blurred Road Map

Consider the challenges faced by a senior manager whose company has been losing market share but who has no certain way to turn the situation around. Or one whose company needs to carry out a number of simultaneous large-scale changes in product lines, information systems, and market strategy but is not confident that the plan for making it happen is really soundly based. Or a CEO who, to keep the company in the race, must transform it into a high-performance, rapid change organization. Or the agriculture minister of a Latin American country whose farms must lower costs and raise productivity if they are to compete.

If senior managers like these want to learn how best to organize a comprehensive attack to deal with such challenges, they will have trouble finding the answers in the published literature on change. One reason is that there are so many articles and books. Moreover, while many of them provide interesting perspectives and insights, they don't provide comprehensive strategies that can serve as strong guides to action. This is true even though many of the writers are top-level thinkers and doers, and many of the experiences about which they write have been bold and highly successful.

The 1982 book *In Search of Excellence* is the wellspring for much of the improvement literature.[1] In it, Tom Peters and Robert Waterman summarized a number of factors that they identified as the keys to success for forty-three companies they regarded as excellent. The authors provided this list of success factors, but they did not convey a workable strategy for becoming excellent.

In the quarter-century since *Excellence*, well over fifteen hundred other business books have been published about making change—five times the number that had been published in the same period before *Excellence*. Virtually all the ones we have seen follow the essential pattern set by *Excellence*, with its strengths but also with its three fundamental limitations:

Backward-looking analysis. All the books describe backwards analyses that offer the authors' ex post facto explanations of why certain organizations succeeded. For example, in 2001 James Collins and his team examined eleven companies that had made a leap from being "good" companies to being "great" companies. In *Good to Great*, he and his team name the factors that, after the fact, were found to be statistically more prevalent in the successful companies.[2]

A large number of the success stories focus on a single company. Jack Welch's *Straight from the Gut*, about General Electric, and Larry Bossidy's *Execution*, about AlliedSignal (and then about Honeywell, which absorbed it), and Andrew Grove's *Only the Paranoid Survive*, about Intel, all exemplify this genre, as, in fact, does Albert ("Chainsaw Al") Dunlap's *Mean Business*. In all these cases the explanations of what contributed to success were constructed after the fact.[3]

Fragmented theories. Most of the key advice that authors provide consists of fragments rather than of coherent strategies. Each author lists three, five, or eight keys to success rather than outlining an overall implementation strategy. There's Peters and Waterman's "seven S's" and Collins and Porras's "big, hairy audacious goals" and Jack Welch's "speed, simplicity, and self-confidence" and Rosabeth Moss Kanter's "enabling the change masters" and Kotter and Cohen's helping key players "see and feel" the need for change and Mitchell, Coles, and Metz's "focus on unblocking stalled thinking," and so on. By the time you've read ten books, never mind fifteen hundred, you are drowning in the "keys to success."

Untested prescriptions. Perhaps most serious, the authors never take the prescriptions they have formulated on the basis of their backwards looks and test them in new environments to see if they really work. All scientific and medical theory similarly begins with hunches and guesses. But no one publishes about scientific or medical theories until they have been tested experimentally. In contrast, the writers on organization change take their thousands of hunches and hypotheses—derived from their ruminations on the past—and offer them as certified "answers."

Moreover, most of the studies studiously ignore the other published work on the same subject. Each presents itself as a pioneering effort into a fresh subject.

One of the few scholars actually to have hypothesized a comprehensive model rather than mere fragments is John Kotter.[4] He has developed a thoughtful and well-elaborated eight-step process for executing change. But, alas, he fails to present the experience of any single organization that has actually employed the process and succeeded.

All of this is not to deny the benefits of reading the literature on change. Many of the ideas and insights are provocative and interesting. And many books and articles share insights on aspects of change without purporting to provide answers. For example, in the late 1980s Michael Beer headed a team at the Harvard Business School that studied a number of attempted corporate transformations, some successful and others unsuccessful. Their book cited the factors the authors identified as differentiating one from the other.[5] Their findings and hypotheses offered novel insights into large-scale change. And the same can be said of Kotter's work and that of Collins and the others cited earlier.

But because the literature consists of fragmented advice and of hypotheses rather than validated methods, managers cannot find research-based information on

- How an organization can best begin the process of change
- How it can keep the process going once it is begun
- How it can tie all the elements of change into an integrated effort

Big Gaps and Big Gambles

This absence of a reliable methodology for large-scale change and performance improvement leaves many managers in a quandary. And management consulting firms have stepped into the breach with huge, big-bang programs. Senior executives, impatient with the pace of progress and having no alternative strategies, are highly susceptible to the idea of home runs and dramatic game-changers. Having no deliberate, controllable process in which they can have confidence, these impatient senior executives grasp for bigger and bigger solutions. These big-bet programs take a variety of shapes and forms. Here are the most common ones:

- *Massive restructuring.* Reorganization, reengineering, and large-scale downsizing offer tempting opportunities for dramatic changes that carry the promise of major bottom-line improvement. Instead of the hard work of organization transformation, these can be done in one sweeping change—often by outside consultants. AT&T's attempt to resolve its problems by spinning itself into three separate businesses is a perfect example. More recently, massive outsourcing and the movement of operations to different countries have become increasingly popular modes of restructuring.

- *Radical strategic shifts.* Enron, an oil and gas pipeline company, sought market mastery through becoming a financial trading company. Vivendi went from being a water company to a media conglomerate. Seagrams transformed itself from a liquor firm to an entertainment company. Westinghouse went from a power equipment manufacturing firm to a financial services company.

- *Large-scale mergers and acquisitions.* There's a plethora of examples: AOL's merger with TimeWarner; Daimler's acquisition of Chrysler; and Chase's acquisition of JPMorgan. Acquisitions promise to produce huge growth steps without having to expend energy getting the current organization capable of new achievements. No wonder they are so popular.

- *Major technology upgrades*. These include huge investments in new technologies, new products, or massive new systems that promise companies the ability to leapfrog the competition. Current examples include customer relationship management systems and the even more comprehensive "enterprise resource systems"—large-scale multimillion-dollar systems projects aimed at bringing together all information about everything into one place.

Unfortunately, the track record of these big-bang strategies is quite dismal. More than half the large-scale mergers and acquisitions of the past decade not only failed to pay off, they actually destroyed shareholder value. Restructurings of troubled companies such as AT&T more often than not created several smaller troubled companies. Massive downsizings and radical reengineering of processes have produced as many downward spirals as uplifting transformations. Moving into totally new business paradigms has been costly for many firms. Many developing countries have adopted programs modeled on the same gigantic big-fix approach as corporations and have created debt burdens that have made their problems even worse.

As if these disappointing results are not bad enough, in many cases the pressure to close the gap has also created ethical and legal issues. Enron, for example, was perpetually pushing the envelope of how fast and how many deals it could create in constantly new areas, even if its people knew little about them. It created a culture where all but the strongest people succumbed to the pressure to do almost anything to succeed, including cooking the books and creating companies that didn't really exist. The same was true of many other companies that chose the crooked road as their shortcut to success. The same with the accounting firms—under pressure to win business and cross-sell with their consulting arms—who went along with client practices rather than question them.

These are not new phenomena—just writ larger in this era of speed and size and instantaneous communication. As we and some others have been writing for decades, senior executives are very frequently seduced by the next new program, the next fad, the next new thing that promises to transform their company. (See, for example, Robert Eccles and his associates' *Beyond the Hype* and Ron Ashkenas's "Beyond the Fads.")[6] With the pressure to succeed driving them to do "almost anything," managers have often grabbed the next big program like castaways drowning in the sea.

Being "Right" Is Cold Comfort

The irony is that in many if not most cases, the big bets that companies, governments, and other organizations make are analytically and logically more or less correct. While some big bets are ego-driven and impulsive, most are based on extensive analysis, financial modeling, and strategic dialogue. They generally derive from thousands of hours of hard work by dozens of extremely bright people—and untold millions of dollars of consulting help. Yet being right is not enough. Consider the following case:

A large electronics manufacturing company, like others in its industry, was being battered by overcapacity, high debt, and a plunging stock price. As part of a turnaround strategy, the company began a massive reorganization to combine its consumer device division with the division providing components to system manufacturers. Financial analysis suggested that this was the right thing to do to reduce costs and "right-size" the company to match lowered business demand. However, the consumer division had a very different set of processes, systems, and culture from those of its sister unit. It was younger and more entrepreneurial, and it had much looser methods and procedures.

Trying to put together these two organizations proved to be far more difficult than anyone had imagined, especially since senior management was hesitant to do anything that would disrupt the way either division functioned. As a result the only actual cost reductions came from eliminating a handful of management positions. The surviving managers, however, ended up with unwieldy spans of control over sub-units—many of which they did not understand. In the meantime, with all the focus on cost issues and the politics of downsizing, the organization unintentionally shifted its focus away from customer service, and many of its service metrics deteriorated. Some manufacturing customers did not renew their contracts. The retail business weakened. Many managers had not yet familiarized themselves with the work of all their units and were not able to react quickly enough to stem the tide. Thus, after almost a year of analysis, consultant studies, financial modeling, meetings, and disruptions, the net result was that revenue losses and restructuring expenses more than offset the cost savings from the reorganization.

This case illustrates how senior managers, driven by the need to "do something," may take decisive actions. But just because the new big plan is right on paper does not mean that it will succeed. For the grand programs to work in practice, the whole organization requires the capability to implement, in a coordinated way, all the changes required to produce the big program's results.

That is why so many of these large-scale catch-up plans turn out to be wrong in terms of results even when the logic and analysis behind them are conceptually sound. That's what happened to the electronics company.

Missing in Action: Implementation Capability

These large-scale change efforts are usually run from the top of the organization, often with the help of teams of consultants, but every one of these major changes necessitates hundreds or thousands of changes at the grassroots level. A change in marketing strategy, for example, may require workaday shifts for hundreds of salespeople who must plan their customer calls differently, submit expense vouchers differently, and make dozens of other adjustments in their routines with customers and colleagues. Multiply this by a hundred or a thousand to get the picture of what is required.

The danger lies in the fact that most organizations are relatively weak in this ability to execute a large number of related changes simultaneously. Nevertheless, very few of the consultants who engineer the massive big-fix change programs ever pay serious attention to implementation capability—other than to complain about their clients' lack of it. Even though implementation capability may be the weak link that breaks their massive programs, they rarely build in any steps to strengthen this capacity along the way.

In addition to needing more basic implementation capacity, organizations need more skill in modifying strategic plans while they are being carried out. As Nadim Matta and Ron Ashkenas point out in "Why Good Projects Fail Anyway," impending changes in the environment, market, customers, and technologies as well as within the organization are essentially unknown at the beginning of a change project.[7] Thus no matter how solid a program may be when it is launched, it will become out-of-date while it is being implemented. Most organizations need much more skill in recognizing these shifts and reacting to them.

Unfortunately, these realities about implementation are all too often left out of the planning of organizational change. In the electronics company case, senior management firmly believed they had the right answer—they had the numbers and analysis to prove it. But the company's managers and staff lacked the capacity to implement it. And no steps were built into the plan either to assess that capability or to strengthen it.

Developing Implementation Capability

The irony is that when people at the organization's grass roots are encouraged, trained, and empowered to act—and given the freedom to make adjustments along the way—they can advance a change process much faster and more effectively than senior leaders and consultants can drive it from the top. For example, in the electronics company described earlier, in the midst of the massive reorganization, the following experiment was conducted: Fifty middle managers and technical specialists were assembled to work on improving the way the company handled "Q Alerts," notifications of quality problems from customers. Over the course of three days, these groups identified nine significant improvement opportunities. They were given the go-ahead to pursue them and were formed into small teams, each accountable for achieving one of the improvement goals.

The teams were given a bit of project management support to help them keep their plans on track, and the senior manager of the area received some modest coaching in how to encourage and empower the teams. In the next hundred days, the teams figured out what would work and what would not, and they learned how to change their plans on the fly. For example, one idea about restructuring the process flow for the Q Alert tickets proved to be unworkable and was abandoned. A new idea that emerged about reducing redundant or multiple Q Alerts turned out to be much more fruitful. So the team shifted its course. In just over a hundred days the nine teams implemented changes worth several million dollars a year. Equally important, they began to develop true implementation capability.

Unfortunately, ignorance of these dynamics—and even contempt for those who pay attention to them—is the rule and not the exception. The consequence is that in the few organizations where the grassroots implementation processes are working well, large-scale change can be carried out successfully. But where infrastructure implementation skills are weak—and that is in most places—the big go-for-broke projects, no matter how well conceived, inevitably fall far short of their potential. This grim reality can be overcome only if, as part of any major change program, serious attention is devoted to strengthening the infrastructure implementation capability. And that is precisely what rapid results projects do.

Rapid-Cycle Projects: Building Blocks for Major Transformation

Rapid results projects are designed to achieve—in a very short time—some actual, measurable results in a strategically important sphere. They are designed also to introduce new ways of accomplishing the work and new ways of managing. Each project of a hundred days—plus or minus—is a miniature organization development step. Each is designed to bring together new mixtures of people and functions and to strengthen work methods and management practices. And each is designed to provide the reinforcement of success.

For example, if the long-term objective is to accelerate company growth, the rapid-cycle projects will aim at achieving some actual growth targets—not just doing market research or product testing or similar preparation. And those projects will aim at achieving their targets in ways that develop better collaboration among functions responsible for marketing and sales, that test new ways to call on customers, that sharpen the project planning skills of participants, that encourage people at all levels to assume more responsibility for achieving results (rather than just doing their jobs). In this way Avery Dennison was able to carry out more than five hundred growth projects involving more than two thousand people in just over a year. Not only were over $50 million of incremental sales delivered in the start-up year, but the company's overall implementation capacity was growing while its culture was shifting into higher gear on growth. (More on this in Chapter Five.)

Rapid-cycle successes are powerful vehicles for developing the grassroots capability to execute major change. Every project strengthens the organization's change capacity a modest but significant amount. All that is needed to make huge gains is to carry out many rapid-cycle projects, over and over, in expanding waves. Each one is carefully orchestrated, and as increasing numbers are run, they blend together into a symphony of change. As implementation capacity throughout an organization grows, and as the confidence of managers increases, the connection between large-scale visions and their grassroots implementation become more understood. Senior management can set increasingly large-scale goals with the increasing knowledge of how to mobilize the entire organization in achieving them. Thus do rapid results projects develop the essential capability that Gary Hamel and Liisa Välikangas call "resilient."[8]

In the rest of the book, we describe how to exploit rapid-cycle results to achieve momentum and to serve as the basis for major change strategies. We also describe how large-scale strategic transformations, to ensure success, must be carried out as a simultaneous blend of large-scale moves in conjunction with myriads of rapid-cycle projects. As you read about these concepts of change, remember these two points:

- While our early hunches and ideas were based on backward-looking, after-the-fact analysis (like the rest of the literature), the methodology that has evolved has been tested and validated and modified repeatedly over many years.

- Because the authors are practitioners first and authors second, the book outlines an integrated, comprehensive strategy for actually carrying out large-scale change, not just fragmentary observations about change.

We begin in Chapter Two by focusing on the fact that most organizations have major resources that are being wasted and not contributing to bottom-line results. These hidden resources are busy canceling each other out or lying dormant in the organization— unsuspected, untapped, and un-demanded. One of the reasons that rapid-cycle projects are so productive and so powerful is that they tap into these hidden reserves and put them to work in new and more productive ways.

Key Points

- Leaders already know they need to accelerate change. They want to know *how*.
- The change literature does not help leaders figure out what to do:

    It includes too many self-proclaimed solutions.

    It offers fragmentary answers rather than frameworks for change.

    It is based on backward-looking analyses—that never get tested in life.

- Lack of reliable methods leads to adopting blockbuster answers—the big bets.
- The big bets—even if logically right—often fail due to lack of implementation capability.
- The rapid results methodology, validated over many years, gets immediate results and develops implementation capability.

2

THE POTENTIAL IS THERE TO RESPOND

Our ancient ancestors saw fire occur spontaneously in nature. Only after they observed it in awe for eons did they eventually realize they could control it and use its power. Rapid results occur spontaneously in that same awe-inspiring way when organizations encounter emergency and must-do situations. We've all seen it happen—a heroic performance in a crisis, an exceptional effort to meet a deadline, an unexpected leap to beat a competitor—and like our ancestors, we've tended to accept it as a force of nature and not something to count on.

The fact that organizations have a tremendous capacity for better performance capacity that can be unleashed rapidly was forcefully demonstrated many years ago. It is a story that we've told many times, so some readers will be familiar with it.

The Bayway Refinery in Linden, New Jersey, then owned by the Esso Corporation (forerunner of Exxon) had been through a 10 percent staff reduction aimed at major cost savings. In trying to run the refinery with the reduced staff of about 2,700, most of the supervisors and employees complained bitterly that the place would not be able to run well. Quality, service, and morale were bound to suffer. This resentment added tension to an already-hostile competition between two unions that both wanted to represent the employees.

The smoldering anger burst forth one day when some of the workers walked off one of the units—leaving it running—as a bit of a demonstration. The supervisors of that unit had to step in and keep it going. In this volatile environment, it didn't take much to encourage other employees to join the demonstration. And over the next day or two, almost all the production workers abandoned their jobs and were outside the plant, demonstrating. Supervisors and engineers by necessity stepped in and took over the operation. Senior management, assuming the demonstration would be over quickly, decided to avoid a costly shutdown. They kept the plant going.

The organizers from both unions got into the act, and insisted on a role in ending what had become in their eyes a sort of strike. Unfortunately for the employees, who had only wanted to express some deep resentment, the dispute dragged on for more than four months. However—and here is the real point of the story—during that time about 450 supervisors and engineers ran the refinery, 450 of the very supervisors and engineers who had been insisting that they couldn't run the place with 2,700 people. Of course, many large maintenance projects did not get done during this period. Nevertheless, the productivity of the refinery at least tripled—with virtually no planning, no preparations, and no investments.

Necessity Is the Mother

As we share stories like this in management meetings, participants always offer new examples. The dramatic experience of the Apollo 13 mission to the moon in 1970 is frequently cited: After an explosion aboard the command module 200,000 miles from earth, speed of reaction was of the essence. James Lovell, one of the astronauts, writes, "A most remarkable achievement of Mission Control was quickly developing procedures for powering up the CM after its long cold sleep. Flight controllers wrote the documents for this innovation in three days, instead of the usual three months."[1]

Such dramatic examples are not that frequent—but small yet equally spectacular occurrences are:

Dorothy Jacobson, who was head of the Microfilm Department at the Morgan Bank, described the phenomenon from her grassroots perspective in a videotape produced by the Harvard Business School.[2] "The Friday before Christmas," she observes, "we always let our people take off at noontime. I never thought about it till I got involved in this video, but on those Fridays all the work gets done before people go home. To do this same amount of work requires a full day the rest of the year."

Some years ago, a freak snowstorm buried Atlanta under nineteen inches of snow. The ceiling of a Mohawk Carpeting plant collapsed, damaging one of the two production lines in the building and putting the other line completely out of business. Within a few days the damaged line was repaired and started up. And within a week it was producing as much as both lines had been producing before the storm.

And, of course, ever since September 11, 2001, the superhuman efforts of New York City police and fire professionals are almost always cited. As people share similar stories that involve various crises—fires, floods, emergency customer requests, and other must-do situations—two profound lessons emerge:

- First, that every organization owns (and is paying for) significant capabilities and resources that never reach the bottom line. They are either obstructed, not elicited, or simply canceled out.

- Second, that in the right circumstances, people in organizations can quickly and spontaneously mobilize grassroots changes and carry them out without benefit of sophisticated planning, higher-level instructions, consulting advice, or training. In other words, rapid results are often, as they were in the Bayway Refinery, a naturally occurring phenomenon.

It was the wake-up experience of witnessing people in many different organizations rising spontaneously to meet new and unexpected challenges that led to development of the processes described in this book.

Zest Unlocks the Floodgates

After thinking about these events and discussing them with others, we realized that some of the things that characterize such events are missing from the daily life of most organizations. They share a compelling urgency to achieve an important result and to achieve it fast. The goal is very clear. People feel a personal sense of responsibility and are stimulated by the challenge. ("Let's show we can do it," they tell one another.) People work together with a new spirit of collaboration. They feel free to modify routines, dropping unnecessary steps and experimenting with what might work better. They have fun.

We call these the *zest factors*. We have asked thousands of people around the globe what they believe enables organizations to perform miracles in crises and must-do situations, and they name essentially the same zest factors as the ones shown in the sidebar. In other words, there is a consistent pattern to these spontaneous events. But for some reason, it is a pattern that everyone recognizes, but few really appreciate.

In Edgar Alan Poe's short story "The Purloined Letter," a police team searches diligently in an apartment for a missing letter. They come back several times when the occupant is away, but never find it. It turns out that the letter they sought had been sitting on a table in plain view the entire time. The police discounted the obvious clue since they were certain that the real letter had to be hidden away, mysteriously.

It is the same with the untapped performance reserve in organizations: it is there all the time. People see it erupting and can

The Zest Factors

Named by thousands of managers as the generators of super performance in must-do situations:

- A sense of urgency—results needed quickly
- Success near and clear
- Personal accountability
- People collaborate—a new esprit
- Pride of accomplishment
- Fear of failure
- Exciting, novel, like a game
- Freedom to experiment and ignore red tape

identify the dynamics associated with it. Yet when managers want to unravel the mystery of organization change and improvement, they instinctively seek out the esoteric approaches and miss the opportunities that are out in plain sight.

You can generate zest and tap into the pool of extraordinary capability locked up in your organization without having a snowstorm, burning down the factory, or suffering a strike. In fact, the reason why virtually 100 percent of rapid-cycle projects are successful is that they are designed to replicate, in a calm and systematic way, the very dynamics that arise in crises. The challenge for managers is to discover these hidden capabilities in their own organizations and to harness them in achieving bottom-line results not just once, but perpetually.

But, asks the skeptical reader, if these resources are so available and require only modest investment to exploit, why hasn't everyone put these ideas to work? Part of the answer is that most managers don't see how such simple-sounding ideas can be relevant for them. Although grateful for spontaneous eruptions of superior performance when they occur, most managers view them as aberrations. They don't realize that they could actually harness all that potential if they knew how to crack the code.

The phenomenon is almost universally ignored or disdained in the writings of the academic gurus and organization researchers. If you read every word ever written about organization change and improvement you would go for a long time before seeing anything about the significance of these spontaneous performance spurts to the practice of management.

Wearing the Blindfold

When we cite examples of zest-produced performance improvements and imply they might have relevance for their own efforts, senior managers and consultants typically respond, "Oh, that kind of outstanding performance can occur for a few days, but then people get fatigued. You couldn't keep it up." Or, "People will only do that in an emergency—but you can't expect them to do that regularly." Or, "There's no trick to that kind of performance improvement. They focus on just the one thing and let everything else drop." And thus do people cast aside the potential insights that these performance spikes could provide.

Why do so many managers seem to be wearing blindfolds when this topic is discussed? We see two reasons:

The first reason is that managers want to feel they are doing a good job—and they want others to believe it also. While they may agree that significant resources are locked up within their organizations, they don't see it as something they can deal with since they are already doing the best they can. They assume that perhaps new methods or new systems or more motivated associates or employees might be the key.

This view is strongly reinforced by the management consultants and academic change gurus who are the main purveyors of the costly big-fix methodologies. As we have written elsewhere, management consultants, particularly the larger firms, simply view the world this way.[3] The solution to organization progress lies in large-scale studies and large-scale projects involving new systems, new processes, big training programs, or big change programs. Big-firm consultants have very little motivation to consider the value of exploiting a company's existing resources in ways that would require much less consulting input. The same is true of many staff experts in technology, finance, logistics, and information systems, who push their technologies in the earnest belief that they are keys to their company's needs.

The second reason for the apparent managerial indifference to exploiting the organization's hidden resources is that there are no handy means for them to do so. Although the tools and methods described in this book are really quite straightforward and uncomplicated, it is highly unlikely that any inexperienced individual could launch the process independently in an organization that has not experienced it.

When the Big-Fix Change Methods Hit the Wall

The net result of these dynamics, as pointed out in Chapter One, is that when senior managers feel the need for major organization performance improvement or change acceleration, they almost always instinctively reach for the big-fix programs rather than focus on what can be achieved rapidly with their existing resources.

Take the example of the Updyke Supply Company (a disguised name).

Updyke Supply, an automotive parts supplier with one center of operations near New York City and another near Cleveland, was suffering from an increasing number of logistical problems. Many orders had to be shipped in several installments for lack of needed parts in inventory. At the same time the overall levels of inventory were well beyond budget, resulting in increased warehouse costs and excessive cash tied up. Some expert consultants were hired to help overcome the difficulties. The consultants carried out a fairly modest study and recommended two changes: an improved sales forecasting system and a modified inventory replenishing system. Compared to many consulting projects, this one was limited in scope and rather sharply focused.

The consultants were engaged to design the plans and to help introduce the new methods. They were also to provide training and instruction to various groups who would be affected by the changes.

In short, to revert to the organ transplant analogy, the logistics "surgeons" were transplanting the new healthy methodology into the company to replace the old failing methods.

Will the transplant take? Let's focus the camera down into two specific locations in Updyke.

- To eliminate the possibility that wishful thinking would influence sales forecasts, the new forecasting system required salespeople to periodically interview their customers, using a detailed checklist of questions. But most of the sales staff felt that they had too

many customers and too little time to spend with each of them.
They were not enthusiastic about what they saw as "wasting
time" on detailed interviews. Moreover, many of them simply
lacked the skill to do the kinds of interviews called for.

- The logistics and inventory unit included two supervisors who
traditionally made certain adjustments to the sales forecasts
based on some unique market information they gathered each
month. One consequence of the consulting project was that
these supervisors were given other tasks to perform in the new
system. No provision was made for them to continue their
adjustment procedure even though the new system did not
adequately deal with the critical variables they had been
adjusting. So henceforth the forecasts would be systematically
skewed.

These were but two small hitches in the grand scheme of
the project. But each of them, to a slight degree, undermined the
success of the new systems. To continue the organ transplant analogy, the "implant" (the new logistics system) was inserted into the
"body" (the Updyke company) without ensuring that all its subsys-
tems would be compatible with the implant. Where there is incom-
patibility between the implant and the ongoing operations of the
organization, as in the two vignettes, the benefits of the new system
will be diminished. Hundreds of such connections have to be compatible, and in Updyke many failed that test.

That's not unusual: when senior managers plan the implementation of major changes they usually pay little attention to possible
weaknesses in grassroots implementation capacity. With the encour-
agement of staff experts and outside consultants, they focus almost
entirely on the overall large-scale change (such as a new logistics or
information system or a new marketing process) and try to drive the
change from the organization's center of wisdom out to the hinter-
lands of implementation. Where the grassroots change ability is
weak—the most common situation—the big-fix projects, no matter how well conceived, will tend to stumble and falter.

Grassroots Implementation
Ability Unlocks the Power

In contrast to the Updyke case, here is an example of another large-scale, strategically important innovation that was carried out by focusing on strengthening grassroots implementation capability rather than through the typical big-fix approach.

The development of complex new electronic devices takes a long time. In what was then the Communications Division of Motorola, new product development was taking an average of fourteen or fifteen months. Many products were taking much longer. To be more competitive, management decided that the process had to be speeded up.

A typical big-fix approach would have been to start with a study of the current process for developing new products. When that was well documented, a new system would have to be developed—on paper. Then, after many months of study and review, the long struggle to implement the new system would have been initiated. Inch by inch the hundreds of formal and informal work pattern changes would be introduced. It could have taken several years, with no certainty of success.

Division management wanted results much sooner than the big fix could be implemented even if everything went as smoothly as possible. A consultant who was helping them suggested that they select an approach that could show some tangible results fairly quickly and generate some zest. By results he meant not a report or recommendations but some actual speeded-up development. On hearing that requirement, some people asserted that the quest was futile in view of the long cycle time for product development. But then one of the development engineers said to the consultant: "Hey, we have two products that we promised would be launched in March—the Syntar X and the Mostar. We missed the date. Then we repromised them for July 1. And we just missed that date. Now we are going to tell the market they will be ready on October 1. Could we use these products for the test?" The consultant asked, "How certain are you of making the October 1 promise date?" "No more certain than the earlier promises," was the answer. "Great," the consultant responded. "That's it. Let's go for it."

The project's goal was to have the two new products ready to release to the market in the promised ninety days. A team of eight people from all the functions involved in development was assembled, with an engineer named as leader and charged with achieving the goal.

In carrying out the project a number of innovations were tested. None was particularly complex—all had been discussed by people at various times but had never been implemented. The most significant one related to work flow. Typically the engineers would do a rough design and create specifications. Then they would pass the product of their work to the design unit, which would refine the engineering specs and send it on to the model shop where they would painstakingly make models. After a few more steps, the manufacturing people received the part. If they saw a reason the part could not be manufactured easily, they would bounce it all the way back to engineering for a new start. And all the in-between work was wasted.

The team immediately realized that they had to change that process to meet the ninety-day deadline. Since they represented all the functions, they decided to examine the design concepts and review specifications as a group and make joint decisions. Thus difficult issues were dealt with by all the functions simultaneously rather than sequentially. Previously each of the functions managed the project when it was in their jurisdiction, then forgot it until it returned. Now the team leader assumed overall responsibility for meeting project goals. A detailed work plan that every function signed on to was created for the ninety-day period, replacing the individual schedules the various functions had maintained for themselves. The new team met weekly with a detailed agenda and would not adjourn until every problem that might delay the process was solved.

Both products were ready at the end of the ninety days. Building on this success, the innovations that the team found most useful were gradually introduced into the division's new-product development system. In much less time than it might have taken just to carry out a

large-scale study and develop a large-scale reformation *plan,* a modified new product development *process* had already paid dividends and
was being implemented more broadly in Motorola's largest division.

This was a rapid-cycle project. It illustrates how such projects
can provide the way to get moving on large, complex programs. It
exploited the hidden potential of capability locked up in the organization. It generated tremendous zest in the pilot team. It illustrates how such projects can introduce new methods and begin to
create the infrastructure development essential to carry out large-
scale changes—even while implementing the first modest project.
The turning point was when management agreed to try this approach,
overcoming the impulse to assert that a modest project like this
could not possibly make a significant contribution to the ultimate
solution.

Not a Hurry-Up Tactical Attack

It should be clear from the Motorola illustration that a well-
designed and well-executed rapid results project is not the same as
a short-term, hurry-up attack aimed at solving a crisis. It is those
narrowly tactical short-term projects—the ones that solve one
problem but do damage in other areas—that have given short-term
focus a bad name. Table2.1 contrasts the disciplined rapid-cycle
project methodology with the typical short-term, tactical effort to
get something done.

The Motorola project is one example of how rapid results projects can make a solid contribution to the development of the organization. This contrast between healthy and unhealthy short-term
projects is also illustrated by Consolidated Edison, the New York
electric power company.

New York City had made environmental cleanliness a top priority.
One of Con Edison's plants had a great number of leaks from valves,
flanges, tank overflows, operating abnormalities, and other sources.

Table 2.1   A Rapid-Cycle Project Is Not a Short-Term Hurry-Up Attack

The Rapid-Cycle Project	*The Short-Term Hurry-Up Attack*
Accomplish the short-term result without sacrificing other goals	OK to drop A for now so long as you achieve B
A stepping-stone to broader gains	Get the immediate result—no matter what
Definite beginning and end	Vague time frame—or none
Pinpointed accountability	Everyone hustling to solve the problem
Deliberate experimentation	Try things out helter-skelter
Planned and disciplined	Trial and error
Learning is built in	Learning is accidental
At the end: Poised for next phase of progress	At the end: Go back and begin to pick up what got dropped along the way

Leaks opened up virtually every day, some of them quite serious. Senior management was adamant: this situation had to be remedied rapidly.

There were literally thousands of ways leaks could happen. How could this challenge be attacked?

- First possibility: A *hurry-up attack* might have been organized by pulling a number of people off their jobs and telling them to find the leaks and fix them—fast!
- Second possibility: A *typical big-fix, across-the board* study of leaks and their repair would have taken many months. Then, at some time in the future, it would have generated a report with hundreds of pages outlining a vast number of solutions that would have to be implemented over many more months.
- Third possibility—and the option selected: A small team was formed to take the lead in generating a rapid solution that the plant could sustain. They decided to start with an experimental

rapid-cycle project for which they set a specific audacious goal: that in the month of May (about two months away) there would be no leaks at all at the plant!

They involved most of the units in the plant in designing and implementing elements of their plan. A number of fairly simple changes in quality procedures were implemented quickly. For example, a number of older machines were known to leak chronically, a fact that had been treated as a bit of a joke. Now, for the first time, the team developed a detailed plan to ensure that each of those machines was turned into a nonleaker. Also, when suppliers delivered liquid chemicals to the plant, small leaks had been regarded as inevitable. But the team decided they were not inevitable, and worked with vendors to create new delivery procedures.

New ways were initiated to communicate to employees about the process and to involve them. With some very modest training in project management, the team was able to organize and implement the entire project. When May arrived, out of its thirty-one days, there were twenty-nine on which there were no leaks. A phenomenal turnaround! And the remaining two days suffered a total of three spills. The learning from this project was the basis for process changes that permanently solved this critical environmental issue.

The Motorola and Consolidated Edison examples show how big, complex issues can be managed through rapid results projects. They also show how short-term projects can be designed and carried out in ways that exhibit none of the sins ascribed to short-term focus, such as dropping an important long-term goal to work on short-term urgency or sacrificing one goal for the sake of others.

In Chapter Three, we describe methods for making these kinds of gains systematically. We outline how to tap into the hidden reserve of performance potential with a virtually 100 percent assurance of success. And we describe how to generate rapid results in ways that quickly build the grassroots capacity that makes ever-larger-scale change possible.

Key Points

- Organizations have tremendous hidden capacity for improvement and change.

- This capacity surfaces spontaneously during crises or must-do situations—when the zest factors are present.

- Most managers, unaware of all the hidden capacity— bet their chips on big-fix programs.

- But the big programs do not take into consideration the hundreds or thousands of grassroots implementation changes necessary for success.

- Building capability at the micro-implementation level is the only way to enable larger changes to occur.

- Project design can ensure that rapid results projects avoid the unhealthy by-products attributed to short-term action.

3

START WITH RESULTS, NOT PREPARATIONS

In the early 1990s, United Aluminum Company in New Haven, Connecticut, had a problem with late deliveries:

United Aluminum management wanted to accelerate the company's growth, but realized that first they had to learn to provide better customer service. With only about 80 percent of their orders delivered on time, for example, they knew they had unhappy customers. And they knew they had to satisfy those customers before expecting they could grow the business. An information systems consultant had been called in, and senior management was about to sign up for the installation of an order tracking system, a typical big-fix attack that was going to cost several million dollars. Moreover, it was going to require that the company tread water for many months while the system was designed and installed. Only after incurring all this expense and delay could progress on improving delivery even begin. It was not a bright prospect.

In another part of the company some rapid results projects had helped speed the output of the company's rolling mill. Could the same approach work for order delivery? With the help of the consultant who had aided in the successful project, they decided to give it a try. The consultant's suggestion resembled the Consolidated Edison leak prevention project described in Chapter Two: Select a week—perhaps forty or fifty days in the future—and aim at having an improved level of shipments during that week. Then, assuming the experiment is successful, apply the learning from it on an ongoing basis.

Since this process offered the possibility of rapid results with little investment, management agreed to try it. But what improvement target to pick for that demonstration week? Some United people suggested a goal of having an 85 percent on-time record that week, up from the usual run rate of 80 percent. The consultant insisted that a more dramatic goal was needed to generate real zest and mobilize the organization, and he suggested a 100 percent on-time delivery goal for that week. Threatening as such a goal might seem, management agreed to it.

With a more modest goal, the company's efforts might have focused on the shipping department, and perhaps included heat treatment, the final operation before shipment. But with a 100 percent goal, it was clear that 100 percent of the company had to be involved.

And involved they became. Every function in the company worked with others to see what it would have to do to support the goal. Dozens of informal task teams were formed (or formed themselves).

Although they were shooting for an apparently impossible goal, a festive atmosphere took shape, almost as if the company were involved in some sort of reality TV game. Music from the *Mission Impossible* television series was played on the loudspeaker system, and "Mission Impossible" hats were provided to all employees who wanted them.

As the target week approached, the whole staff worked hard to do their part. When the week finally came, 100 percent of the orders were delivered on time. But when the game was over, what would happen? Although no commitments had been made beyond the model week, people nevertheless kept working in the mode they had designed for the model week. After all, it represented their idea of how the work really should be done. During the following week 100 percent of the orders were also shipped on time. Since that experiment, on-time deliveries in United Aluminum have never been lower than 95 percent.

Some modest changes were needed in the company's order processing systems, but for a relatively minor cost—and not the multiple millions for the order tracking system that was proffered as the ideal choice at first. The British Broadcasting System aired this project on *Business Matters* in 1993.

In 2004, thirteen years after this project was carried out, the United Aluminum Web site emphasizes on-time delivery as a key selling point. The company's recent "On-Time Shipment Scoreboard" is shown in the sidebar.

United Aluminum:
On-time Delivery Record

2002	2003	2004
99.1	98.9	98.9

Tactics Atypical

This on-time delivery project is an example of what is possible when management is willing to free itself from the straitjacket of the big-fix view of the world. Since the company had tested the rapid-cycle process already, its managers were game for trying it on a more ambitious goal. They understood something of what could happen by tapping into the intelligence, capability, and readiness of their people to generate progress toward a tough goal.

By contrast, most improvement efforts in most organizations consist of big-fix strategies (similar to the Updyke experience cited in Chapter Two). These efforts rely for success on the wisdom of the strategy and the energy of senior management in implementing it. But success in these efforts is always limited by the organization's grassroots implementation capability: its ability to carry out the hundreds or thousands of individually minor changes needed to support the overall large-scale change. If those capabilities are well honed, an organization can absorb large-scale change rapidly. But if they are not, there will always be severe limits to what the organization can achieve.

Unfortunately, the latter is the more common scenario. Most change and improvement efforts in both the developed world and the developing world tend to be of the big-fix variety, driven by consulting programs or massive reengineering and the like. Success in implementing these changes is limited by the grassroots change capacity of the organization—which often turns out to be much too little compared to what is needed. Worse, these big-fix change processes usually have no provision for helping the organization develop implementation capability while the big change is being carried out.

Perhaps the most extreme example of this focus on big-fix strategies for change is in the realm of large-scale economic and social development. Institutions such as the World Bank, USAID, the United Nations, and regional development banks invest billions of dollars each year in well-meaning large-scale change efforts. Often developed by economists and technical experts, these ambitious plans for poverty elimination, social development, education, and the like very often founder on the shoals of grassroots implementation capacity within the countries they are meant to improve. And, as with similar projects in individual businesses, they fail to develop the basic implementation capacity within the country that would allow large-scale efforts to succeed.

By contrast, as the United Aluminum case demonstrates, a rapid-cycle project not only exploits the hidden resources in the organization to achieve results quickly but also strengthens the grassroots implementation capability. The organization benefits from a combination of quick paybacks and the development of capacity for long-term gains—a truly benevolent cycle. And that, in a nutshell, is what rapid results is all about. *A rapid results project is a focused effort that can generate zest, that can be achieved quickly, usually seventy-five to one hundred days, and that yields a successful result with tangible rewards while simultaneously providing a developmental breakthrough for the organization.*

Let's begin to show in more detail what these projects are and how they can contribute so powerfully to an organization's progress.

Rapid-Cycle Projects: The Reinforcement of Success

The United Aluminum case illustrates the three beneficial outcomes that a rapid-cycle project achieves (shown in the sidebar).

First, it yields positive payoffs almost immediately. A very modest investment of resources produces economic dividends within weeks. People quickly begin to see change efforts as successful, self-funding mechanisms—rather than as sinkholes for endless investment in improvements that are always promised for the future. Moreover, the reinforcement of success is a shot of adrenaline to all the people who participate and to the leaders who help the process get moving. That provides an important psychological boost. In fact, in almost all cases, rapid results projects improve morale and confidence.

This boost can occur even in distressed companies:

For example, a utility plant was being deregulated, and everyone knew that it would soon be for sale. Management launched several hundred-day projects to improve plant maintenance, and this helped unionized employees feel that they were doing something to make the plant more attractive for potential buyers—thus increasing the likelihood that they would still have jobs after the sale. In other words, the projects helped them feel that they had greater control over their destiny.

Benefits of Rapid Results Projects

- Fast positive payoffs
- Work process innovations
- Learning and development

The second benefit is that rapid-cycle projects generate all kinds of process innovations. In preparing for the model week at United Aluminum, dozens of experiments in new ways of working were designed and tested. Innovation was the order of the day, and people began to feel free to participate in designing different ways of working. Thus the rapid-cycle project can be designed as a living laboratory to test process innovations, not as abstract ideas but as tools that are immediately applied in achieving urgently needed results. The sidebar on page 36 summarizes a few of the kinds of innovations that can be tested.

Third, every rapid-cycle project yields important gains in new learning and development. As with the United Aluminum staff all

Sample Process Innovations for Rapid-Cycle Projects

- Adopting project management disciplines
- Sharpening results measurement
- Setting one-person accountability for results no matter who is involved
- Engaging lower-level associates in innovative projects
- Making tougher and more explicit demands
- Forming temporary teams to creatively attack a task
- Adopting business process mapping and process redesign
- Applying quality management techniques
- Using cost analysis
- Experimenting with customer and vendor partnerships
- Making economic value-added experiments
- Collaborating across organization boundaries

striving to achieve the 100 percent on-time delivery goal, rapid results projects require people to take on new responsibilities and to experiment with new ways of working with each other. They have to face up to the full accountability for results (instead of just giving it a good college try). This experience of assuming new responsibilities, taking new initiatives, and implementing a wide range of innovations provides lessons about making things happen that are new for everybody.

And in those three outcomes lies the power of the rapid results project—the confidence-building payoffs, the process innovations, and the learning and development that expand everyone's capacity to manage change

These outcomes set the stage for expansion and acceleration of the process. As each project is completed, it serves as a building block for larger-scale change.

Developing the Capability to Support Large-Scale Changes

Beyond strengthening the organization's basic implementation capability, rapid-cycle projects can create the processes and the readiness that enable organizations to successfully carry out large-scale changes.

The United Aluminum on-time delivery case describes how the many rapid results projects designed to meet the challenging 100 percent on-time goal not only achieved the result but also demonstrated that the large order tracking system that was to have been installed was not needed. It helped to identify the kinds of simple systems changes that would be useful, and it helped to develop the capability of the company's people to implement and use these modest changes. The hard work of actually achieving the 100 percent delivery goal provided important learning to virtually everyone in the company. Thenceforth, any major project involving several units in United Aluminum would be carried out with much more confidence, sophistication, and grassroots initiative than ever before.

Contrast this with the way most big-fix projects are implemented by management consultants. Hordes of consultants move through the organization, making exhaustive studies, preparing detailed recommendations that spell out the new ways to do various jobs, advising people on implementing the new system, and making adjustments to it. The attitude of these change engineers about the organization's people is reminiscent of the joke by a theater person about a puppet show she had been managing: "The puppets have done a perfect job at the last few performances—but they are not quite ready to do it on their own." Given the way many large-scale changes are carried out, it is no wonder that an organization that goes through such changes is no more ready to tackle the next project than it was the previous one.

Designing a Rapid-Cycle Success: A Disciplined Process

To achieve the objectives of both results and capability development, rapid results projects need to be carefully selected and designed to meet the seven key criteria listed in the sidebar on page 38.

Important Goal

To gain attention and devotion to success, a rapid results project must be aimed at something that everyone, from senior managers

Criteria for Designing Rapid Results Projects

- Focuses on an important goal
- Produces a measurable stretch result
- Works in the short term
- Pinpoints clear accountability
- Drives experimentation
- Is planned and disciplined
- Makes learning a deliberate outcome

to shop-floor workers, will recognize as important. It cannot be carried out as a mere exercise but must be seen as part of a high-priority business imperative.

As a result, rapid-cycle projects need to be clearly linked to, or in alignment with, some key strategic objective of the firm. The Motorola project cited in Chapter Two focused on speeding new product development; the one in Con Edison focused on environmental cleanliness, and United Aluminum's project focused on on-time delivery. They all focused on critical goals. This is in sharp contrast with the "employee involvement" or Quality Circle initiatives of past years, which encouraged employees to select change projects that they wanted to work on.

These projects illustrate how rapid results projects can move companies forward on large, critical strategic dimensions. In this way they can serve as low-risk, low-investment thrusts into new territory that provide rapid testing of large-scale strategic directions. These rapid results projects sometimes also generate enough momentum to spawn new strategic directions themselves.

Andrew Grove, chairman of Intel, describes this phenomenon in *Only the Paranoid Survive:*[1] "Assigning or reassigning resources in order to pursue a strategic goal is an example of what I call strategic action. I'm convinced that corporate strategy is formulated by a series of such actions, far more so than through conventional top-down strategic planning."

Measurable Stretch Result

To produce a sense of victory and stimulate the adrenaline rush associated with the zest factors, it is critical that a rapid-cycle project produce a real, measurable result—and one that is beyond what would have been considered possible. This is the very opposite of the "low-hanging fruit" tag that is often hung on rapid results projects by those unfamiliar with the concept. Picking low-hanging fruit teaches organizations nothing about performance acceleration. Achieving unprecedented gains teaches much.

Often, the first learning occurs with the seemingly simple act of identifying the goal for the first project. It is essential to select a goal that will yield a real, tangible result. If quality improvement is the long-term goal, it is necessary that the rapid-cycle project produce some actual improvement in quality. Reject rate down. Yields up. Customer returns down.

Groups often start by selecting goals like "introduce a new way to measure quality." Or "develop an effective quality training program." Or "establish a new quality inspection process." Or "Highlight the reasons for quality problems." No. All of these may be good things to do, but not one of them is a measurable improvement of quality—and thus none can provide the reinforcing stimulation of a real result.

Similarly, if sales volume improvement is the ultimate goal, the rapid-cycle project needs to generate an actual, measurable increase in sales. Not conduct market research. Not develop a new advertising campaign. Not have Marketing, Sales, and Manufacturing agree to work more closely. All these might be built into the project, but none is a real sales volume increase, and that is what *results* means in a growth project.

The experience of a telecommunications manufacturer illustrates the shift in thinking needed to get into the "measurable results" frame of mind.

The company was running out of capital partly because its inventory was way out of control. The situation was dire. A consulting firm was installing a totally new inventory control system, but the work was not slated to be completed for at least another seven or eight months. In a true big-fix frame of mind, operating managers said they were powerless to do anything about reducing inventory until the new system was in place because they didn't even have accurate information on inventories.

Senior management, eager to make progress sooner, asked a consultant for his thoughts. He asked them whether it was true that every single category of inventory was beyond control. Was there any kind of inventory for which they did have a decent measure? The operating managers allowed that there was one category for which they had exact figures: that was "SNA inventory," which meant "shipped but not accepted." This was equipment that was on the customer's premises, perhaps even being used, but not paid for because of some unresolved quality or contract problem. Voilà! A results-focused project that could be started at once: reduce the SNA inventory by a significant percentage within the next few months.

Not only did that project begin to reduce inventory, it provided an important warm-up exercise in the eventual installation of the full new system. By contrast, a project aimed at studying SNA inventory or recommending solutions, no matter how potentially useful or how rapidly accomplished, would not qualify because these are not results.

At the same time, it is not enough that the rapid-cycle project produce just any result—it must truly be a significant step up, a stretch beyond what could be accomplished simply by working harder. Participants need to gulp and gasp when they hear the goal—and realize that it cannot be achieved by doing more of the same but only through experimenting with doing things differently. In the United Aluminum story cited earlier, going from 80 percent to 85 percent on-time delivery would have been a worthwhile achievement, but it would not have spurred company-wide energy and innovation. But with the goal set at the seemingly impossible 100 percent on-time delivery level, everything was called into question, releasing a tidal wave of innovation and energy that would not have appeared with a lesser objective. Rather than plucking low-hanging fruit, participants have to figure out how to harvest the fruit from the topmost branches—and do it quickly.

Short Term

To capture and exploit the zest factors—and to create the kind of spirited, high-energy determination that the United Aluminum folks developed—a short-term perspective is essential. To us short term means anything from a few weeks to three or four months. Many projects use a hundred-day time span. Some years, ago when consultant Rodney Blanckenberg first adapted the process to loading eucalyptus logs on flatcars in South Africa, he coined the title "100-day action projects."

How can this requirement be met when the goal that management wants to work on is a large-scale goal that might take many months or years to achieve? The key is to carve off from the large goal a slice that can be achieved in the hundred-day period. In the Motorola new product development example cited in Chapter Two, considerable creativity was needed to decide to focus on getting the two late products out into the market in ninety days.

A short-term focus completely changes the dynamics of a project. It is almost impossible to arouse much zest with a twelve- or eighteen-month project. But to achieve results in a hundred days or less, action needs to start virtually at once. The team needs to pull together quickly, figure out a plan of action, test new ideas right away, and get on with it. If teams were allowed an additional three or four months, none of this urgency would be generated.

A group of Siemens Corporation managers decided to design and launch a new maintenance service to augment their manufacturing business as their rapid-cycle project. When they sketched out the steps they might take, and all the approvals and tests that would be needed along the way, it looked like at least a fifteen- to eighteen-month project. Instead of investing all the time and effort required to set up a full maintenance business, they set a goal of a pilot effort that would actually write some orders within four months. Their success on the pilot then produced the evidence that a new business would indeed be viable.

To carve out a rapid-cycle goal from the overall business opportunity, we suggest the use of a funnel diagram (Figure 3.1). The overall opportunity is written down at the top, and the team's job is to select a subgoal that meets the criteria. In the first diagram, a large-scale goal of increasing market share in the NAFTA geographic area was carved down to a specific sales increase of specific products in a specific region within twelve weeks. In the other diagram, a chemical company had to reduce the cost of manufacturing a key product or it could not compete. The overall cost reduction goal was carved down to one specific productivity gain in two months.

Note that the subgoal is not just step one toward the big goal (such as doing a study of the situation). Instead, it represents a complete mini-project that yields a tangible result.

Clear Accountability

Many projects fail because of multiple accountabilities and lack of clarity about who has what accountability. In a rapid-cycle project, accountability must be very clearly defined. Usually one person, the team leader, is the ultimately accountable person, no matter how many other people from however many functions need to be involved. While that person may share responsibility with other members of the team, the ultimate accountability is always clearly allocated to the one person. As soon as more than one is accountable, the possibility for ambiguity slips in.

This clear accountability for an actual result also contributes to stimulating the zest factors. Someone who is on the hot seat and really has to deliver just naturally acts with greater urgency, energy, and persistence. Really accountable rapid-cycle leaders do not let organizational barriers and constraints stop them and their teams. Instead they create pathways to success—over, around, or through the barriers!

In the Motorola new product development case, this requirement proved to be difficult to implement. In the development of new products,

Figure 3.1 From Overall Objective to Rapid Results Goal

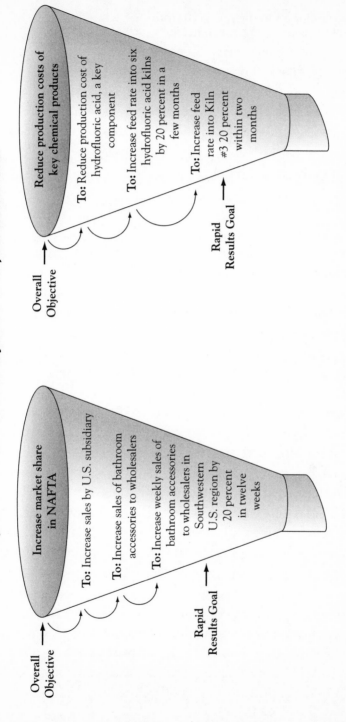

each function had autonomy for what went on within its walls. It was pointed out to them that no one had overall accountability for the development project. But when one-person accountability was suggested, they shot back: "How can an engineer see a new design through into manufacturing? He knows nothing about manufacturing." Eventually their rapid results project did test a single accountable project manager working with a multifunctional team. That approach proved so successful in this project that it very quickly became the standard procedure.

Experimentation

Rapid-cycle projects are meant to test innovative approaches to achievement. The entire spirit of the rapid-cycle project must be experimental. The basic premise is that the project not only yields a result but also tests new ways of working and of achieving results. That is why the requirements of measurable stretch goals and short time frame are so critical: they force people to deal with the fact that acceptable results will not be achieved by working in the same old ways.

The experimentation often is encouraged by new combinations of people—from different functions and levels who together have the requisite talents and experience. Some of the most successful teams we have seen were composed of radical new mixes of people—such as production workers on teams with sales reps and lab scientists. In a rapid results agricultural project in Nicaragua, for example, the team included representatives from the government's Ministry of Agriculture together with local farmers, academic agronomists, executives from a dairy company, and agricultural extension agents—a critical but never-before-attempted combination.

In every organization people have ideas about different ways to get things done. But one deadly effect of poor grassroots implementation capability is the absence of easy ways for people to test their innovative ideas. Most people rarely think of experimenting because their organizations provide few opportunities for anyone to experiment actively. Rapid-cycle projects offer abundant opportunities for experimentation and thus encourage people to keep thinking about another way to get something done.

In one nuclear power plant, for example, a series of innovative job planning methods were tested in a project to reduce the number of costly delays in maintenance jobs. In the electronics company described in Chapter One, a hundred-day project to reduce the frequency of quality-related Q Alerts also led to the creation of a much more rapid way to prioritize new systems projects.

In encouraging the conduct of hundreds of rapid-cycle growth projects, Avery Dennison managers told their people to select projects that not only would yield immediate growth but also would force them outside their comfort zone. This was meant to ensure that they would use the projects to venture into new, innovative territory.

Planning and Discipline

While freedom and experimentation are critical, the projects are not free-for-alls with everyone doing their own thing. On the contrary, a critical characteristic of a rapid-cycle project is careful planning by its team. Steps are thought through; written work plans are laid out with a relatively clear schedule; tasks are explicitly assigned to individuals.

Because of the pressure to get results quickly, some teams are initially reluctant to create disciplined work plans. They want to just get on with the work. But some simple, nonbureaucratic disciplines are essential. When the time frame is short, teams cannot afford to miss a step or to assume that something is getting done when it is not. Thus having plans in writing, keeping the plans up-to-date, and organizing weekly reviews are all essential. Moreover, as more and more projects are undertaken, these disciplines become absolutely crucial.

GlaxoSmithKline's IT function, for example, insists that all business systems applications projects pay for themselves within one year. This requires each project to include rapid-cycle pieces that demonstrate measurable business payback in a few months. Since many of these projects require fast-moving collaboration between various IT functions and business users, often in different parts of the world, project leaders are required to employ a suite of electronic project management tools, accessible to all team members through the company's intranet. After some initial resistance, project leaders soon learned that using these tools allowed them to coordinate actions with people in different locations much more effectively than before, saving significant amounts of time.

Deliberate Learning

The rapid-cycle project aims not only to produce the immediate result but also to serve as a springboard for expanding progress. It is important that each project be treated as a learning laboratory to provide data on what works. This learning needs to be an explicit dimension of the project. Explicit learning goals for the project and the kinds of learning that may be possible need to be defined at the same time project work plans are being developed.

One important learning element derives from the fact that participants serving on rapid-cycle projects generally keep their regular jobs going at the same time. Therefore they learn how to get more done with the time and resources available. Senior managers who care about their people sometimes relieve them of some or all of their other tasks when they are assigned to a project, saying things like, "We want to be certain Beth has all the time she needs to make the project succeed." But this kindness undermines one of the key learning opportunities—how to shift time spent on lower-value-added work to higher-value-added work. If people are relieved of other tasks while engaged on a project, this learning may never occur.

Those are the seven criteria that ensure both the immediate tangible results from the project and also success in the developmental aspects of the project.

Yin and Yang

It should be obvious that in extolling the power of rapid results projects we do not propose them as an alternative to longer-term vision and strategic management. Rather they are a necessary, complementary element in major strategic change efforts. So many large-scale changes introduced into the organization are essentially rejected—much as organ transplants may be—and they do more harm than good. Rapid results projects ensure that the large-scale strategic efforts are absorbed into the organization.

Rapid-cycle projects, as illustrated in Figure 3.2, are the keys to linking implementation at the grass roots with the large-scale changes. As the two types of change feed each other, it makes for true organization development and advancement.

Figure 3.2   Continuous and Expanding Progress

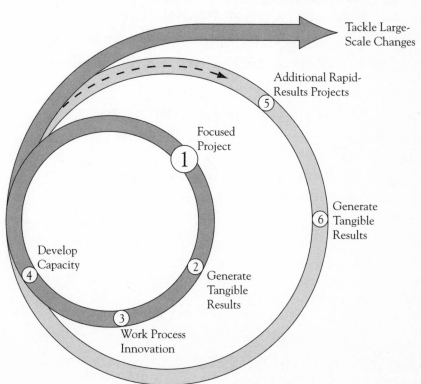

Subsequent chapters focus not only on how to use rapid results successes to develop infrastructure capacity but also on how this strengthened infrastructure makes it possible to carry out successful large-scale change. In other words, they show how to create a total change process that exploits the power of rapid-cycle projects as a critical dimension of organization progress.

Part Two, beginning with Chapter Four, illustrates how these projects can deliver rapid paybacks and simultaneously develop the infrastructure implementation capability of the organization.

Then, in Part Three, we illustrate how the development of change implementation capability provides a powerful base upon which to construct far-reaching strategic change and major performance improvement.

Key Points

- Rapid results projects strengthen grassroots implementation capability and test large-scale change in low-risk ways.

- They begin with action and results, not preparations.

- Rapid results projects need to be carefully designed to provide both results *and* learning—thus setting the stage for expanding scope.

- These short-term projects complement—and do not replace—long-term efforts.

Part Two

RAPID RESULTS

Expanding Implementation Capability

Part Two describes how rapid-cycle projects capture untapped energy and creativity and put them to work in achieving significant bottom-line results. These results are often way beyond any normal expectation of pace or achievement. And while the organization is enjoying the benefits of these results quickly, it is also expanding its power to manage larger-scale change by engaging large numbers of people in improvement and by creating its own unique architecture of change.

4

GAIN RAPID RESULTS
ON KEY GOALS

There is no manager in any organization in the world, in any function or role, who can't find opportunities right now, today, to organize and launch some rapid results projects that will accelerate progress toward critical goals. Current operations offer never-ending opportunity for gains that can go right to the bottom line while they build implementation strength.

The first opportunity to test rapid results and build high levels of change capability is right where you are now—in your current operations. But this is not an academic exercise—you don't start by saying, "Oh, let's try some rapid-cycle projects." The place to start is where you see impatience or dissatisfaction—some real urgency to change what is happening. A promising new product that is not getting into the marketplace fast enough. Cycle times that need to be speeded up. Product modifications that are taking too long to carry out. Large-scale organization realignments that are too slow.

Cash When You Need It

When facing challenges like these, the most difficult hurdle is to free yourself from the pedantic paradigms of organization improvement and get going on achieving improvement. For example:

ROBERT A. NEIMAN and HARVEY A. THOMSON, lead authors; Catherine V. Beavan, Rudi A. Siddik, and Claudio Avila Tobias provided case material.

Banorte, the third largest bank in Mexico, was having difficulty providing service in its 2,500 automatic teller machines. ATMs had physical breakdowns, unstable communications lines, or innards jammed by old bills, or they were out of cash or vandalized. These were causing a total of 5 percent of lost time for customers (ATMs available only 95 percent of the time). The situation was not just losing money for the bank, it was irritating the customers, and the last thing Banorte wanted was dissatisfied customers.

Management was attempting to overcome the problems by upgrading software, negotiating with the central bank for better-quality bills, training branch personnel, negotiating faster response levels with maintenance providers, and requesting more resources for new technology. The assumption was that once all the individual problems were overcome and all the elements were functioning smoothly, ATM reliability would go up. But the results never came; people had too many different goals to pursue at once and no process for integrating all their individual efforts. Moreover, many of the responsible people felt they were doing all they could and that further improvement would require more resources.

When it was suggested that they focus on a small segment or territory to test some improvement ideas and learn what it would take to increase availability, Banorte managers were quite reluctant. The country-wide problem was so urgent that a small pilot effort seemed too trivial. However, since the progress they were achieving with their other approaches was not nearly fast enough, they decided to try it. They narrowed the focus down to one neighborhood in Mexico City that had forty-four ATMs, just about 2 percent of the Bank's total machines. The goal was to reduce inefficiencies in those forty-four machines by 60 percent in thirty days, which would mean increasing availability from 95 percent to 98 percent. Prudencio Frigolet, the head of ATM operations, convened a team representing all the related functions—measurement and control, branch operations, central operations, cash replenishment, and maintenance service providers—in a two-day action planning event.

In their planning session, the team broke down the ATM problems into causes related to physical condition, data communications, money replenishment, and vandalism. And, for each of the most recurrent and highest-impact problems, the team devised a strategy. For example, they would sort and feed bills by grade to eliminate jams at ATMs. They would dedicate a SWAT maintenance team to tackle breakdowns more quickly. They would deploy basic repair kits and critical components using mini-cars as mobile warehouses to roam the city.

At the end of the session the team received approval from the territory director of Mexico City and set about implementing their recommendations. They conducted weekly meetings to launch and follow up on the actions, to review progress, and to hold each other accountable for carrying out their assignments. The Control Department set up an online report of the forty-four ATMs so people could see day by day how their actions were affecting performance.

At the end of four weeks, the outcomes revealed to Frigolet the power of the rapid results project. Availability reached 98 percent from 95 percent; in other words, 60 percent of the downtime had been eliminated. Process innovations had been introduced like the sorting and feeding of high-quality bills and delivering cash based on predictions of use rather than a fixed schedule. Team leaders made it their business to carry out their tasks without stopping at the traditional organizational boundary lines. These dramatic outcomes and the psychological reinforcement of success set the stage for expanding the process.

Even before presenting the results to the territory director, the team decided to look at the rest of the ATMs in Mexico City. Frigolet analyzed the ATM performance for each area of the city and explored with the local people whether the same process innovations could work. They selected new area leaders and new teams. These teams set a more challenging goal: to increase the availability of the remaining four hundred ATMs within ninety days. That was ten times the number of machines included in the first project with only sixty extra days budgeted. When Frigolet asked the team leaders, Maria Fernandez and José Juan Flores, how they decided on that new goal, they responded: "The team feels so confident with what was learned that they now want to try the whole city at once."

The territory director gave them the go-ahead. At a one-day planning session the original team assisted the new teams from each of the other areas to plan their strategies, based on the learning captured during the first implementation cycle. A similar weekly review process was then set up between the new teams and the original team. The expansion strategy started to show results after forty-five days of implementation: ATM availability rose from 95 percent to 97.7 percent in northern Mexico City, and from 93.3 percent to 98.3 percent in the southern part.

After the expanded Mexico City project was completed, Frigolet understood what could be achieved by tapping into the intelligence, capability, and readiness of the people to generate progress toward a more ambitious goal: the national ATM network. Almost in parallel with the conduct of the Mexico City expansion, he asked Flores to work with his IT managers to assist the branches from each region in implementing the easiest and highest-payoff actions, "those not requiring any resources," as Fernandez put it. For instance, each branch closely followed the procedures to track and replenish money for each ATM under its responsibility.

Within the next few months, the 2,500 ATMs across the whole country were up 2.5 percent in availability year-over-year, from 94.9 percent to 97.4 percent: "These are figures we have never seen before . . . and so rapidly," Fernandez added. In less than twenty weeks from start-up, the outage time of 2,500 ATMs throughout Mexico was reduced by about 40 percent—and it has remained at that level.

When we suggest that managers consider rapid-cycle projects to accelerate progress in their organizations, we often hear a retort similar to Banorte's initial response: "Are you kidding? We have big changes to make, huge changes. We can't waste time on small pilot efforts." But, as the Banorte case illustrates, the first successes come quickly and create the capacity for accelerated progress. Then expansion can be very rapid.

The value of the overall Banorte gains can be estimated from this: after four months it was calculated that the gains on the first forty-four machines—2 percent of the system—were worth US$300,000 per year. Had Banorte leadership insisted on keeping their focus on the big goals, they might still be waiting for progress to begin.

Banorte continued to use this approach in other areas of the bank. Within the first year, those projects delivered annual benefits of US$7 million per year.

New Recognition for Implementation

The ATM project exemplifies the kind of progress that any organization can make. You might think that your company is doing everything that can be done to improve performance. But the truth is, it is not. A hard look at any organization always reveals plenty of opportunity to be exploited.

Increasing numbers of authors are pointing to the importance of implementation in operations. Some management thinkers regard it as a critical component of strategic advantage. Michael Hammer, in his article "Deep Change: How Operational Innovation Can Transform Your Company," points to the extraordinary success of companies that have elevated themselves to world leadership status in operational implementation—Toyota, Dell, Wal-Mart, and Progressive Insurance, among others.[1]

Hammer says, "Compared with most other ways that managers try to stimulate growth—technology investment, acquisition, major marketing campaigns and the like—operational innovation is relatively reliable and low cost." It is also completely under management control. "So why don't more companies embrace it?"

Hammer then delves into the change barriers he encounters. "The answer hinges on some unpleasant characteristics of contemporary corporate leadership. Business cultures often undervalue operations—cast it as low in status, boring, unglamorous. Many senior managers, schooled in finance, strategy, deal making, and marketing, simply don't know much about operations—leaving it to the engineers."

Robert Hayes and his colleagues, in *Operations, Strategy, and Technology: Pursuing the Competitive Edge*, strive to bring operations out from under the shadow of performing only a "support role."[2] They, too, cite the power of operational excellence and innovation. They go further to point out that such gains don't occur just because managers agree to the need for such improvement and keep the pressure on. The organization requires a strategy and process for such change. Hayes, too, points out the inherent barriers of insufficient change capability. "A number of studies have shown that about two-thirds of such programs 'fail' in the sense that they don't produce the results expected."

The dot-com boom of the '90s encouraged the fantasy that great dreams could come true by dancing on the head of a pin. When that balloon was punctured, it made people realize what conservative citizens believed all along: to achieve success it is generally important that you do something that others value and that you do it well. In the years following the dot-com bust, the concepts of excellence and of performance efficiency and, more specifically, of implementation, have been emphasized once again as critical ingredients for success.

Psychological Barriers Inhibit Implementation

Beyond Hammer's explanation, we believe one of the reasons that many organization leaders seem to undervalue the importance of implementation capability in their quest for success is that they lack sufficient confidence in their ability to generate it. A surprisingly large number of people reach senior management positions without extensive experience in getting their troops to tackle very difficult challenges successfully.

When those managers face a tough goal, many fail to stand up in plain sight and say to their people, "This is what we have to do;

now let's decide how we're going to do it—and by when." Instead, they slip into a variety of alternative routines and processes that are part of their organization's traditional modes of attack on goals. They focus on doing the preparations and studies that simply *must* be done before they can decide how to move. They feel that if the goal is a critical one, they'll need some major help from consultants to provide experienced guidance. They look for additional staff or budget to get the job done. Most organizations have an endless supply of such delaying tactics to postpone action in favor of preparations.

Do managers consciously do these things? No, most of these maneuvers are done unconsciously by managers who really want to succeed and want their organizations to succeed. The lack of real confidence in their own implementation capability, however, gives rise to hidden anxieties. Once they take a public stance about achieving a goal, their reputation is on the line. Their people may tell them that it simply can't be done. Support functions may not be able to provide needed support. For all these reasons it can be a bit threatening to be the publicly named, accountable manager for a project with a very challenging stretch goal.

But it can also be rewarding, fun, and exhilarating. This chapter outlines a wide variety of ways to get started using rapid results projects—in both operations (such as costs, quality, sales) and so-called soft areas (such as worker safety, morale, culture).

The Different Ways to Get Started

The place to begin is with something you feel must be improved. If you want to test the rapid-cycle approach to improving results, we offer three principal ways for selecting a goal and achieving it:

- *Straight performance improvement project.* This is a project that aims at an incremental performance improvement that is viewed as a stepping-stone toward large-scale improvement.

The Banorte project that focused on forty-four ATMs in a neighborhood of Mexico City is an example.

- *Process redesign project.* Where the large-scale redesign of business or work processes is a major theme of an improvement effort, this type of project carves off an isolatable element of redesign that can yield some measurable gains quickly. *One Northeast Utilities generating station had a poor record of meeting commitments in routine maintenance work. A multifunctional team mapped and redesigned the process for coordinating manpower, equipment, supplies, and approvals with the goal of having everything come together at the appointed time for at least 95 percent of routine maintenance jobs.*

- *Model week (or model month) projects.* We have discovered that groups of people are willing to strive for unbelievable levels of performance for a short time as a kind of experiment. Then, once they have successfully achieved these so-called impossible goals and understand how those levels of performance can be sustained, they are willing to accept much higher new norms. *The United Aluminum project cited in Chapter Three shows how powerful this approach can be.*

Thinking in rapid-cycle terms is a whole new way to approach goals. Because it is different from many people's well-entrenched way of thinking, it definitely takes a bit of getting used to. Most managers treat the creation of a new set of plans or a new system or a new training program as a result. They have difficulty in limiting the definition of *result* to real, measurable outcomes like costs down, sales up, turnaround time reduced. Table 4.1 provides a catalogue of actual rapid results projects that have been carried out. This list may help stimulate your thinking about how to define a rapid results project in your own organization. After you have been through the process a few times you will quickly get the feel of how to carve out a results-focused project no matter how large, complex, or elusive the overall goal may be.

Table 4.1   Rapid-Cycle Projects in Operations

Organization	Critical Business Goal	Rapid-Cycle Goal
Manufacturing Effectiveness		
Grupo Industrial Saltillo	Cost synergies in corporate procurement	Reduce cost of top four common materials (safety supplies, pallets, packing materials, chemicals) by 25 percent by the end of March.
DuPont Canada	Plant cost reduction and productivity improvement	Increase proportion of packaging film slit to size in-line (rather than off-line) from 52 percent to 70 percent in three months.
Customer Transactions		
Canada Life Assurance Company	Increase new business and improve customer service	Speed turnaround time for processing new group policies so that 80 percent are completed in twenty-five days or less.
PNC Financial	Get all quarterly statements out on time and error free	Eliminate by 15 percent the error and late rate in retail account statements in the Philadelphia bank in twelve weeks.
Financial Operations		
Federal Reserve Bank of Philadelphia	Improve operating cost performance rank from #11 to #3 in the system in nine months	Eliminate redundant forms and paper supply inventory by 20 percent in eight weeks.
Information Systems		
PNC Financial	Install totally new deposit accounting system in all banks in two years	Install deposit accounting system in three banks in three months.
Logistics		
Grupo Industrial Saltillo, Mexico	Rapid returns on new acquisition	Achieve $600,000 in cost savings through purchasing and operations synergies within seventy-five days.
Mining		
U.S. Borax	Reduce costs	On the 4100 shovels, reduce lost loads due to shift change from twenty-eight to eighteen by April 30.
Hamersley Iron, Australia	Increase capacity of ore-carrying rail system	Reduce by thirty minutes the time required to recouple trains after emptying them, within six weeks.

Customer Partnering:
Rapid Results Across Boundaries

When the success of any one group or organization depends on working more effectively with other groups, a cross-boundary rapid results project can generate the needed momentum. Such projects involve people from different functions or units within an organization. Sometimes companies use these projects to forge stronger links with customers and suppliers for the benefit of all parties.

All the advantages that accrue from a rapid results approach are multiplied when applied to customer partnering—immediate improvements in operations, quicker resolution of customer issues, and better customer satisfaction and relationships. Designing a rapid results project with a customer, however, is a slightly more complex undertaking since it involves mobilizing two organizations in the shaping, launching, and implementation of the project. Success also depends on tapping the hidden reserve and overcoming the barriers to performance improvement in two distinct organizational cultures.

The following example illustrates how one supplier was able to reach out to a major customer to jointly improve their delivery process and to reduce costs.

Bronson Schafer, senior account manager of U.S. Borax, a global supplier of borate products, was concerned about finding competitive advantages for his basic commodity product—borates.

"It was at a time when many organizations were under extreme pressure to reduce costs," Schafer explained. "Purchasers targeted pricing for their contribution to their company's cost reductions. At the same time, U.S. Borax was carrying out similar cost-reduction initiatives with the hope of a somewhat healthier bottom line; having to adjust prices downward could easily negate those imperatives."

Moreover, Schafer was concerned about retaining customer commitment. One of the company's large customers was particularly dissatisfied with delivery of borate products. So Schafer proposed a partnering effort to improve delivery performance and to reduce costs for the customer. While the customer's global sourcing manager tended to ascribe the delivery problems to U.S. Borax, he was willing to go along with a first step, at least. He was pleased that U.S. Borax was willing to take some initiative on the issue.

The first effort was called the "materials replenishment break-through project." The objective was to streamline ordering, transporting, and replenishment processes to ensure that adequate supplies of borates were available at customer sites at all times. Such a project, if done in the traditional way, would have involved five or six months to conduct a study, another six months to gain customer approval, and then endless months for implementation. Instead, U.S. Borax and the customer decided to try the rapid results approach to get the project under way quickly.

Within a week, a joint team was formed to work on this project. The customer's team consisted of representatives from Purchasing, Transportation, Quality, and Operations; the U.S. Borax team came from Distribution, Transportation, and Quality. Co-leaders from each organization were given a written assignment from Schafer and the customer's sourcing manager that outlined the objectives of the project as mutually agreed by both companies.

"This kind of work demands resources from both parties," Schafer said. "On one hand, a greater sense of value is appreciated when both invest equally. On the other, and perhaps more important, there are things we can only accomplish together." The main ground rule was that any action by the joint team had to benefit both the customer and U.S. Borax, the supplier. Projects had to be win-win for both companies.

The team launched their work a week later. As members shared their internal processes with each other, there were a number of surprises. For example, the U.S. Borax people had not been aware that at any given time four to five of their railcars, fully loaded and idle at the customer's site, were being used as just-in-case inventories by the customer even when their silos were full. Similarly, the transportation groups found out that they were both expending a lot of time and effort in tracking the same railcars across the network with the various railways.

The team decided to focus initial attention on the long transportation cycle time that was causing delays in deliveries. The first breakthrough goal was to reduce the transportation cycle time to one of the customer's sites by 25 percent. They committed themselves to achieve the goal within three months. This meant reducing the cycle time from twenty days to fifteen days from the time a railcar was loaded at Boron, California, to the time it was unloaded into the customer's silo in the Midwest.

With this goal in mind, the team analyzed the bottlenecks in the transportation process and brainstormed ways to improve the flow of railcars through the network. For example, one of the major bottlenecks was near the customer yard itself, since these shipments involved handling by two railroads, Santa Fe and Union Pacific. The joint team developed a detailed work plan to combine their resources and expertise to resolve the transportation issues with the railroads. They developed new procedures to ensure that railcars, once unloaded, were returned quickly by the railroads to U.S. Borax. The net result: the transportation cycle time was reduced by the planned 25 percent—and in a month and a half, not three months.

Following this first success, the team focused next on improving the overall ordering and replenishment process at this customer site. The next breakthrough goal was to achieve specific savings in time and expense in this process for both parties. The teams decided to reengineer the process into a consignment arrangement whereby U.S. Borax became fully responsible for automatically replenishing the silos at the plant.

This arrangement eliminated non-value-added activities for the customer—placing orders, tracking shipments, and processing invoices—as well as reducing paperwork from these activities. It also eliminated the need for both companies to do tedious quality inspection and testing for each shipment. And U.S. Borax was relieved of the need to prepare Certificates of Analysis and invoices. Borax's team expanded to include production planning, information technology, legal services, and accounting to help build the supporting systems and infrastructure to make the consignment process work effectively. They piloted the new consignment system at this one site and then rolled it out to the other sites in North America.

This breakthrough project generated savings of hundreds of thousands of dollars annually for both organizations. The customer was no longer burdened with inventory costs and ordering expenses. The improvements to the supply process enabled U.S. Borax to free up at least twenty-five railcars (the ones that typically sat idle in the network under the original system) for other customers. In addition to these tangible savings, a new relationship of mutual trust and respect emerged from successful collaboration between U.S. Borax and this important customer.

As Bronson Schafer put it: "This collaborative work helped U.S. Borax and our customer to focus on delivery and excessive costs incurred in each transaction. Additionally, technical teams worked together to reduce waste and improve productivity in their plant operations. This customer partnering program was brilliantly successful and proved to be a seminal moment, in that we have expanded the offering to a broad spectrum of customers who see value in it. It has become an important feature of the way we do business with our customers."

This case illustrates how all the criteria described in Chapter Three need to be carefully built into the design of a rapid-cycle project for customer partnering. As with projects carried out within a single company, joint projects must

- Provide a clear benefit to everyone involved.
- Have very clear accountability for success.
- Focus on a real measurable result.
- Encourage careful planning and execution by the team.
- Encourage experimentation and new ways to work together.

That's the winning combination in hard business areas. But it also works in soft areas as well.

Attaining Hard Results in Soft Areas

The same results-focused approach that produces dramatic improvements in hard dimensions of business priorities—revenue, cost performance, profitability, quality, and customer service—is equally effective in achieving measurable improvements in the soft areas of organization performance. Those areas include worker health and safety, employee diversity, job flexibility, organization culture, corporate image, communications, and employee satisfaction.

Untold billions of dollars are expended on activities related to such goals, and more billions are lost as a result of failure to address such goals competently. For example, the U.S. Department of Labor reported that there were 4.7 million nonfatal injuries in private industry in 2002, a staggering 5.3 cases per 100 full-time workers. More than half of these resulted in days away from work, or job transfer or restrictions, costing U.S. industry many billions of dollars. On another dimension, class action suits for discrimination in employment, compensation, and promotion have cost individual companies settlements in the hundreds of millions of dollars.[3]

Despite these astronomical costs, very few companies are satisfied with their accomplishments in this area.

Why Are Hard Results So Elusive in Soft Areas?

One reason that results are difficult to achieve in the soft areas is the same underdevelopment of implementation capability that plagues improvement initiatives in hard performance areas. These soft areas are harder to pin down and thus are even less susceptible to big-fix, top-down cures. In addition, some unique barriers hamper results achievement in these soft areas:

- *Soft goals don't seem key to business performance.* Managers may not make the connection between poor performance in soft areas such as health and safety, diversity, and employee involvement on one hand and the company's bottom-line results on the other.

- *Self-defeating goals are set.* Managers know they should address these soft issues, but often set goals so lofty and visionary as to provide no impetus for change or guidance for action. "We will become the employer of choice." "We will be the most innovative company in America." Goals such as these fail to produce a sense of urgency or clear guidelines for action.

- *Results measures are weak or absent.* There is some truth to the maxim, "What gets measured gets managed." Unless soft areas have ongoing performance measures like the ones for market share, inventory turns, and product quality, they won't get the attention or the results.

- *Accountability is diffuse.* Usually no one individual or function has total responsibility for achieving the improvement in soft areas such as diversity or worker safety or turnover. And when accountability exists at all, it is too often for *activities* (get a program under way) and not *results* (reduce accident frequency by x percent).

- *Too much reliance on staff functions and outside consultants.* Many seasoned managers see their jobs as delivering the hard business results and feel that issues such as organization culture, diversity, employee satisfaction, and health and safety, while obviously important, are really extras. They are more than happy to turn these issues over to staff specialists or to outside consultants.

Even if only some of these barriers are operating in a company, it can make success unattainable.

Rapid Results in Employee Diversity: The Citigroup Europe Experience

The rapid results approach places the responsibility for results squarely on line managers. Using rapid results projects to address soft performance areas ensures not only that measurable results are produced but also that implementation capability is developed.

Citigroup epitomizes a company driven to achieve hard business results. Earnings per share and ROI are the watchwords of corporate success. However, past efforts to diversify Citigroup's leadership, such as diversity conferences, awareness training, and building networks, did not command the same attention from the company's hard-driving executives as revenue growth or profitability. Lynne Fisher, director of diversity for Europe, decided to use rapid results projects to launch a sustained initiative to enhance the diversity of the leadership group. After gaining the commitment of the senior management of European Operations, she set up cross-functional, cross-business project teams to make measurable progress on diversity within a hundred days.

The teams set goals for recruitment, for sponsorship and career development, and for retention, work-life balance, and respect. The recruitment team, for example, set a goal to increase from 30 percent to 40 percent the number of women applicants for investment banking positions. The work-life balance team set a goal of having twenty-six employees from one function working at home within a hundred days. Goals such as these enabled the project teams to create and test out various solutions and learn what it takes to achieve and sustain mea-surable improvements in diversity.

By building in scheduled progress reviews, Citigroup brought the same management disciplines to diversity that it employs in its banking businesses. Further, these reviews signaled senior management's con-tinued interest in the issue. The participation of various high-potential employees on the project teams was a development experience in its own right and provided the team members with career-enhancing visibility.

These projects not only produced results, they generated a sense of excitement about the possibilities for improvement. With each breakthrough success, more managers grasped the idea that diversity and inclusion goals are amenable to a more businesslike approach. Initial successes helped pinpoint changes that needed to be made in various human resource management systems—recruitment, develop-ment, assessment of management talent—to achieve comparable results across the corporation. For example, diversity performance has become a core component of managers' annual performance appraisal. As part of an annual talent review, Citigroup has added a "deep reach" assessment several levels down in the organization to ensure that diverse talent is getting the kind of developmental experience early in their careers that will equip them to compete for senior-level opportunities.

Keeping Connecticut's Health Workers Healthy

The experience of Connecticut's Department of Mental Health illustrates how organizations can build on rapid results successes in soft areas to sustain and expand higher performance levels. Some years ago, the department was alarmed by the growing number of employee injuries caused by interactions with patients—including assaults. These injuries not only undermined employees' physical well-being and morale, they also drove up workers' compensation costs.

Sincere but uncoordinated initiatives to correct the problem (introduced by hospital administrators, medical staff, and the unions) were having little impact. No one in any hospital had overall responsibility for reducing incidents of assault, nor did anybody have an overall picture of how various factors were interacting to increase patient distress, a major contributor to assaults on staff.

In a low-risk, low-investment way, two wards in one hospital, Fairfield Hills, were selected to pilot a rapid results approach. Multidisciplinary teams set a goal of reducing incidents by 10 percent in a few months. For the first time ever, the doctors, nurses, attendants, and others who worked in the wards collaborated in a joint undertaking. They analyzed patient incidents and assessed the possible relationship between medication, nutrition, patient-handling practices, restraining equipment, and ward culture and the occurrences of incidents. They examined which patients were causing the incidents and whether the incidents showed any other patterns. As the team discovered the key factors, they tested a combination of remedial strategies. They discovered that certain patients caused most of the incidents, and that most incidents occurred at certain times of day. They were able to alter the

focus of employees on the wards to respond. The result: they significantly overshot their goal, reducing the incidents on the two wards by
60 percent. When extended to all six wards in the hospital, the year-
over-year reduction in staff injuries was 75 percent, reducing the workers' compensation cost by a significant amount.

This approach was adopted by a second hospital in Norwich with
equally dramatic results. To sustain the results-focused improvement
effort, the hospital trained internal facilitators, both management and
union, to support rapid-cycle projects throughout the hospital—and,
ultimately, throughout the state. A sister department, Mental Retarda-
tion, applied this results-focused approach statewide as well, reducing
its workers' compensation costs by over $10,000,000 per year. This
Connecticut story is described in more detail by Suzanne Francis and
Matthew McCreight in "Restoring Health to Workers Compensation."[4]

It's Not Rocket Science

Citigroup and Connecticut's Mental Health and Mental Retarda-
tion departments and many other organizations have achieved
measurable gains in soft performance areas by exploiting rapid
results projects. In doing so, they have followed essentially the same
formula as the one for achieving rapid results in hard goals. For
many managers it seems less natural to use these disciplines in
attacking the soft goals. Nonetheless, although defining the measurable goal may require a bit more creativity in the soft areas, the
tasks are essentially the same and the success rate is just as high.

Rapid Results Projects
Create an Execution Culture

As an organization carries out more and more successful rapid-cycle
projects, a culture of execution evolves. People become more willing to tackle goals—both short term and long term—and more
competent in achieving them.

A number of years ago, for example, Fred Poses, who went on to become the chairman and CEO of American Standard, was general manager of a plastics materials division of AlliedSignal. Poses wanted to accelerate growth of his division, but with no financing available for expansion, he would have to get more mileage out of his current resources if he wanted to grow. He decided to begin by focusing on one set of extruder machines. He challenged his manufacturing manager and the extruder team to get more quality production. Putting their heads together, they quickly sketched an approach to achieve a 25 percent increase in output from one set of extruders in about six weeks.

The manufacturing and extruder teams worked every day on the project. They discovered they had to reduce the changeover and cleanup time between runs, which meant a different changeover routine. It meant having cleaning supplies and spare parts immediately at hand. The maintenance department took responsibility for this. They discovered they had to get the warehouse to provide more raw materials every day, which in turn meant a faster order cycle from suppliers and more storage space near the extruding machines. The purchasing and warehouse people took on that task. They learned they needed more frequent lab tests and faster lab response to assure on-spec quality at the higher output rate, so they asked the lab people to do that.

Dozens of other improvement ideas were identified and introduced. Doing all this in a six-week time frame was a whole new experience for everybody involved. The project demanded a lot of ad hoc experimentation. They learned as they bumped into roadblocks each day and worked creatively to find ways around them.

By the end of six weeks, the whole system was actually beginning to work at the expected level. People discovered they could get the same old machines and the same old people and the same old facilities to produce much more without new investment.[5]

But much more was accomplished than the productivity boost. In achieving the results, people changed their views about what might be possible. "We no longer needed to spend time arguing about why it can't be done," Poses explains. "There's a culture of let's give it a try and see."

The six-week push for the 25 percent output increase had produced a basic shift in the culture of the extruder operations as illustrated in Table 4.2.

With the success of this project, and the shift in attitudes,
Poses and his people began to apply the same approach to other
improvements, and thus to generate the momentum needed for
the expansion.

The Rewards Are Worth the Effort

You get the idea. It's the job of managers to make things better.
Rapid-cycle projects provide a way to exercise that responsibility.
Each project yields a dividend of learning: how to select the best
goal; how to generate interest and motivation to act on the goal;
how to create a strategy and do the problem solving needed to
come up with a workable strategy; how to generate cooperative
effort and overcome obstacles and diversions; how to integrate various efforts needed to get the results; how to reward success; how
to manage such projects to put maximum reliance on the people

Table 4.2   A Changing Culture

From	To
Change as a special project run by a special staff team	Change as an inherent part of the job of the operating people
Each function working only on its own tasks	Joint responsibility for shared objectives
Sequential work flow—study, then pilot test, then evaluate, and then implement	Parallel work flow—study, pilot test, evaluate, and implement as virtually simultaneous actions
"Prove-it-first" attitude	Experimental, "let's try it" attitude
Diffuse accountability	Accountability focused on the manufacturing managers
"We need more resources to get better results."	"We must get better results with what we already have."

who do the work. Each project can help overcome common dysfunctional syndromes—and bypass the perpetual preparations.

But what if you need to launch many projects at once and get many people across the whole organization working on critical improvement thrusts? In Chapter Five we discuss how to mobilize large numbers of people into change and performance improvement work very quickly.

Key Points

- Every manager has opportunities to accelerate progress with rapid results projects—starting today.

- Better operational implementation itself can be a competitive advantage.

- Rapid results projects can be used to improve current performance, strengthen collaboration with customers, or attack soft goals such as diversity and worker safety.

- Rapid results can help create a culture of operational success and implementation excellence.

5

MOBILIZE LARGE NUMBERS OF PEOPLE IN CHANGE

It is not uncommon to hear business leaders make statements like, "We have too much going on to undertake any more projects for a while." If you were to probe what is actually happening you would find that "too much going on" often means that the usual suspects—a small number of able senior people—are drowning in special assignments and one-time projects while the rest of the organization goes about its routine work. Naturally, if the same fifteen or twenty people are exclusively the keys to change, they will also function as the limits to change. To develop truly superior implementation capability it is necessary that large numbers of people at all levels share responsibility for making change occur. When hundreds or thousands of people are mobilized, the potential multiplies many times.

This chapter shows how rapid results projects can serve as a vehicle for engaging large numbers of people in the change and improvement process. Further, it describes how a modified version of the well-known GE Work-Out process provides a structured methodology to support this rapid engagement.

Accelerating Corporate Growth

In 2002, the top managers of Avery Dennison concluded that its then-current approaches to stimulating growth would not achieve their intended results. At that time the company, which specializes in office

---

MATTHEW K. McCREIGHT, lead author; Elaine M. Mandrish provided case material.

products and adhesive materials of all kinds, had an annual volume of just over $4 billion, with more than twenty thousand employees around the world. The company enjoyed enviable profitability levels, but it had grown less than 10 percent over the past two years even though growth was a top management priority. A number of productive acquisitions had been made. Every division was concentrating on developing new products. And the Corporate Strategy and Technology function had been providing extensive support to the divisions as well as funding new product projects that looked promising. But the results were still not adding up to what was needed and what had been promised to the investment community.

One of the steps senior management took to accelerate progress was to make an inventory of the kinds of growth efforts under way in the company. That inventory made abundantly clear that virtually all of the company's growth activities were focused on longer-term activities—such as the development of new technologies and new products. These were efforts with two- and three-year lead times. Very little effort focused on achieving near-term growth by exploiting products and technologies already in existence. This was not surprising; many business leaders throughout the company were certain that they had pretty well saturated their markets with the current products and available technology. So it was no revelation to discover that growth to these people meant new products for new markets.

When CEO Philip Neal and President Dean Scarborough saw how little was being done on immediate growth (which they called Horizon 1 or H1) they saw an opportunity.[1] They realized that any H1 successes would generate results in a short time with little investment. They were confident that there was more opportunity out in the world than their managers were recognizing. Moreover, since the longer-term growth projects engaged only a small number of employees—mainly in marketing and technology—H1 might engage many others.

They decided to test how they could generate growth very quickly using products and technology that the company already possessed. Three divisions in the Cleveland, Ohio, area were selected for a pilot experiment.

The Pilot Projects

The managers of each of these divisions were asked to do some creative thinking and to select some potential new business opportunities that might yield results within one hundred days and *also* have the potential for much larger gains in the future. In this case *results* meant actual additional sales or at least the chance to make a proposal to an interested customer. In the three divisions, fourteen growth opportunities were targeted.

One project, for example, focused on expanding the business done by the company's Specialty Tape Division. This division manufactured a foil product used in heating, ventilating, and air conditioning applications. They decided to offer a tape version of that product, along with a companion product that they had to outsource. Their goal was to have both products available, with appropriate packaging and labeling, and actually on the shelves of one large U.S. distributor within the hundred days. Success opened the possibility of about $2 million per year of additional business.

In another division, one project was designed to speed the entry of a competitive new in-mold labeling technology to market. Introducing the technology had been seen as a long-term effort, because the sale required that customers invest in automated application systems that would be added to their production lines. Marketing officers in the division felt that they would need to build a complex cost-benefit model and establish relationships with several automation suppliers before they could take the technology to customers. But a small team of sales, engineering, production, and marketing professionals set themselves a goal of securing letters of intent from two large customers within a hundred days.

For each project an interfunctional, multilevel team was assembled and charged with responsibility for achieving the measurable results. Team members had to keep their regular jobs going at the same time. Some of the projects were led by people from Sales, others by technical or Marketing managers. The teams included people from R&D, Operations, and even staff functions like Legal—whatever was required to achieve significant commercial results within the time limits. There was some consulting assistance, but it focused on getting the process moving and not on providing the growth ideas: the growth ideas and creativity came from the team members themselves.

The results achieved during the first hundred days were remarkable. One team closed within fifty days on a sales target that had been scheduled to come in over the course of twelve to fifteen months. Another team designed and developed a product solution previously considered impossible—and got customer approval at a price that represented a breakthrough in profitability. A third team, in addition to developing certain automotive components that they would supply, took the initiative to act as a kind of coordinating broker—integrating the contributions of a number of other suppliers for a critical product line for one key customer. In addition to helping the customer solve an urgent problem, the team more than doubled sales on the Avery Dennison components in this customer's product line.

At the end of 2002, the company's top managers traveled from Pasadena, California, to Cleveland to attend a report-out on the pilot teams' hundred-day experiences. Virtually every one of the teams reached its numerical growth goal. Equally important, the sixty people who had participated on the teams were enthusiastic about the experience. One technical manager said that the rate of learning on his project was the fastest in his twenty-four years at the company. A long-term sales manager said that in all his years he had never had the kind of exposure to how the "rest of the company" really worked as he did while leading a cross-functional team to secure a $2 million commitment from a customer. CEO Philip Neal called the meeting one of the "most exciting days I can remember" in a long career at the company.

Rapid Expansion

After that review session, President Dean Scarborough, with strong support from Neal and other senior managers, decided to expand the process across the company beginning at once. The outside consultants created some guidelines for selecting and launching projects and helped to get the roll-out process started. Beginning with operations in the United States and Canada, at each location a high-potential manager was designated to serve as "growth champion." The champions' job was to assume the role of internal consultant in spreading the program in their divisions. The outside consultants helped launch the process in each location and helped the growth champion develop the know-how needed to lead the process. Once the major U.S. sites were moving, priority turned to Europe, where the same process was used. Then it was Latin America. And finally, Asia, Australia, India, and South Africa. In each case the outside consultants helped introduce the process but focused mainly on helping the growth champions take command.

Helen Saunders, head of a European division, was appointed vice president of growth initiatives, reporting to Scarborough, with the job of leading the H1 efforts throughout the company and coordinating the work of the growth champions. Saunders and her champions became a sort of internal consulting firm who developed and extended the H1 process with constant innovation and experimentation. One critical example: A number of H1 teams had spontaneously experimented with new ways of collaborating with customers. With a hundred-day time frame, the old way of having a salesperson or technical representative act as the sole go-between with customers was much too slow. A number of H1 teams recruited staff members from customer organizations to join their teams; other teams went as a group to visit and work with customers. Very quickly it became apparent that these innovative methods encouraged unparalleled collaboration and customer support. Some customers became so enthusiastic about the hundred-day spirit that they launched their own hundred-day projects. Saunders and the growth champions made certain that these customer collaboration innovations were captured, shared around the corporation, and built into the work going forward.

The process was supported by the company's Corporate Communications function. Diane Dixon, its head, made sure that explanatory bulletins and letters, videotapes, posters, and a wide variety of other devices made it certain that every Avery Dennison employee anywhere in the world would know about the process.

The basic implementation strategy budgeted very little time for formal training for team participants. Rather, the aim was to capture some of the know-how and creativity that already existed, untapped, throughout the corporation. Prospective team leaders attended a half-day orientation session, as did the people who were to be team facilitators. Each team sponsor—the senior manager who was the ultimate "client" for each team—also received a few hours of orientation. It was intended that additional skill development would occur as one dimension of the team work sessions. The assumption was that learning would be a by-product of successful experience rather than injected into people up front. Senior management encouraged learning. CEO Phil Neal repeatedly said, "Our growth process is a giant learning experience—and we are all learning together." One of the selection criteria, for example, required that projects "push participants out of their comfort zones."

The project teams selected a wide variety of approaches to achieving incremental sales in a hundred days: by getting to market faster on targeted growth opportunities that had long time frames; by partnering with customers to develop product modifications that would meet unique needs; by finding new markets for old products; by modifying old products for new uses; by providing unique value-added services that would enhance the customers' benefits in dealing with Avery Dennison, and many other techniques.

Gratifying Results

The initial pilot projects were conducted at the end of 2002, and the company-wide rollout was launched at the beginning of 2003. During that year it was introduced into more than fifty sites around the world. With the rapid results methodology it wasn't necessary to write off 2003 as merely the "get-started year." Just the opposite! Avery Dennison's 2003 annual report tells the story:[2]

> In 2003 we commercialized the first products created by our
> Horizon 1 program—a fast track process in which a team is

given a 100-day deadline to solve a specific problem in order
to meet a customer's need. The revenue generated in 2003
by these Horizon 1 projects reached approximately $50 million
in annualized incremental sales. We have found that there is
a certain psychological magic associated with a short 100-day
timeframe, which sparks a sense of urgency and high energy
among team members. There are currently about 550
Horizon 1 teams hard at work creating and seizing new
business opportunities . . . with more than 2,300 employees
serving on them.

From a standing start, within a year more than five hundred projects
and more than two thousand people around the world were actively
involved. As Terry Schuler, senior vice president of HR, described it,
"Dean did a great job in managing this all the way through. Think
about it. The roll-out for H1 began at the beginning of 2003. And by
the end of 2003, everyone was doing Horizon 1 around the world.
That is really something."

Building on the momentum, toward the end of 2004—the second
full year of H1 activity—Tom Van Dessel (who had replaced Helen Saunders as the head of the H1 program) reported that the company was
on track to record over $150 million of incremental sales resulting from
H1 projects during the year.

This Avery Dennison experience demonstrates that large numbers of people can be engaged in a change and improvement
process very quickly, generating significant performance results.
Without huge up-front investment in endless preparations Avery
Dennison got moving at once toward results. Skill development,
innovation, new methods, and other innovations were not ignored;
they were built into the work of achievement. As the Avery Dennison case shows so dramatically, it is the very act of striving for
results and achieving them that can serve as the culture-changer of
all culture-changers.

As Dean Scarborough puts it:

> The hundred-day deadline drove an incredible amount of creativity. When people hit obstacles, they did not come to management for help. They realized they were working against a very tight deadline and they did what they had to do to get over the obstacles. They took some risks. I think that is good. Even in markets that we considered to be quite mature, when we went out with an H1 project, we found ways to grow. Because we were getting closer to our customers and partnering with them on the H1 projects, we found new ideas for what they needed that we could supply.

And Terry Schuler adds:

> H1 projects interconnect the functions. This is most critical with the sales force versus the inside people. In the past, the sales force tended to look at the rest of the people in the company almost as if they were from a different world. By working with people from other business functions on H1 teams, the sales force has developed deeper appreciation of what it takes to get the job done inside of the company. Just as the salespeople got closer to the inner workings of the company, the flip side of that is that finance people, HR people, marketing people, and manufacturing people all got closer to the marketplace and gained a better understanding of what is required to sell products to customers. The H1 process with its interfunctional teams gets everyone out of their silos. It builds a collaborative understanding across functions.

And the short-term results were also contributing to an empirical, action-oriented approach to strategic direction-setting. As Dean Scarborough puts it,

> In terms of longer-term strategy, the H1 process allows you to test big strategic concepts very quickly and in a very focused way. If you have ideas about things that you want to do in terms

of new products, new customers, new services, new geographies, you do not have to spend forever doing a long study. Even when you finish one of those studies, you often don't really know how much you can rely on it. If you go out and test the idea in a small-scale hundred-day way, you have some real solid data. We have been able to implement certain strategies much more quickly this way.

Senior Management Involvement

It is important to note that Phil Neal, Dean Scarborough, Bob Malchione (senior vice president of corporate strategy and technology), Terry Schuler, and Helen Saunders (as well as other senior managers) all devoted a certain amount of energy to supporting the effort. One or more of these senior managers were represented in a great many of the fifty- and hundred-day team project reviews all over the world. At each of these reviews, six or seven teams, each with five to eight people, had the chance to tell their proud stories to senior management and to interact with them.

Picture, if you will, a production operator with more than twenty-five years of service in a Belgian plant, standing up to report project progress to Dean Scarborough, Helen Saunders, the heads of his division, and about thirty fellow team members at all levels. He was able to report that he not only helped to revive a mothballed piece of equipment so that a certain modified product could be produced, but he also figured out how the machine could be made to yield double its published production standard.

It Seems So Easy.
Why Doesn't Everyone Do It?

If the process is as straightforward as described, and the results so substantial, why haven't more companies tried it? The answer is that while it is straightforward and simple to describe, it is hard work and even a bit threatening to carry out. Chapter Two described some of the psychological barriers that get in the way. In addition, for corporate leaders to undertake the kind of experimentation that achieved so much for Avery Dennison it is necessary for them to take sword in hand and exorcise the self-defeating myths that drive them into the arms of the big-fix change purveyors. Here are the four most common of these myths:

- The idea that change is so formidable and resistance so universal that extensive, costly preparatory activities must always be carried out before change is attempted. These include all of the big-fix preparations—training, reorganization, codification of strategic plans, culture changes, creation of the right attitudes about the impending changes, installing the new information systems, and so forth.

- The "father knows best" syndrome—the belief that because change is so complex the most powerful group of brains in the company need to design and control the process. Many of these leaders say they'd like everyone in the organization to participate in the changes, but they seem trapped in the conviction that they need to be out leading all the change. This drives them to become embroiled in specific, detailed operational changes that are often outside their area of expertise.

- The view that focusing on rapid results is shortsighted. This is the classic myth that has stood as a timeless barrier against rapid-cycle experimentation. The big-fix fantasy—"To make big change, you have to think big"—belittles small-scale efforts as being too trivial.

- The notion that the larger the organization, the longer it takes to get change moving. This drives the conclusion that in the biggest organizations it is ridiculous to expect change to happen quickly.

The Avery Dennison experience—as well as the many other examples in this book—gives the lie to all these self-limiting and self-defeating myths. With more than twenty thousand people working in forty-four countries around the world, Avery Dennison nevertheless got the entire organization on the march within a year. Virtually no preparatory work was needed in the business units to get the H1 projects launched and succeeding. People throughout the company, at all levels and in all functions, were able to respond with ingenuity, enthusiasm, and wisdom.

The Work-Out Process:
For Mobilizing the Entire Organization

At Avery Dennison, the process of mobilizing the entire organization began with the targeting of some very specific improvement opportunities in each part of the company. As each opportunity was identified, a project team was created to achieve a specific results goal related to the opportunity. In almost all divisions, it was deemed more important to gain some quick momentum and embed the methodology than it was to select exactly the right projects to work on. Since successive waves were going to be launched one after the other, it didn't matter if the absolutely best projects weren't selected in the first round—they would be selected in the second or third. And the very process of tackling some worthwhile results rapidly generated significant learning about where to go next.

Nonetheless, organizations often do find a need to involve much larger groups of people in the launch of a major performance improvement or change effort. In these situations, a modified version of GE's Work-Out process can be an effective tool for success. The process generates action just as quickly as the team-based rapid-cycle approach used by Avery Dennison, but does so by assembling larger numbers of people and having them select the areas for action. This is especially appropriate where specific goals and priorities are not clear and where multiple functions or organizations need to collaborate to develop effective solutions.

Work-Out was developed in the late 1980s by General Electric. The company had changed dramatically over the preceding years—

selling and buying businesses and significantly reducing the size of its staff. But with the old ways of working still in place, people were bogged down by bureaucracy. It took too long to take action, and the company was losing touch with customers.

GE started Work-Out with a fairly narrow focus—as a method for eliminating bureaucracy and redundant work. Over time, Work-Out broadened to business processes, then to customers and suppliers, then to change acceleration. By the late 1990s, Work-Out had become the foundation for the company's push into Six Sigma. At the heart of these efforts was a basic focus on driving change in rapid increments and building ever wider involvement and capabilities among large numbers of people.

Several authors of this book were part of the original team that helped GE design and roll out the process across the company. Since then, the methodology has been adapted to focus more on measurable results, to involve more people at all levels, and to drive change in very rapid cycles. This experience has been captured in *The GE Work-Out*.[3]

How Work-Out Works

Work-Out involves people and empowers them to put their ideas, energy, and creativity to work in making the organization successful. The power of the method is that large numbers of people, frequently more than a hundred, can all participate at once in the rapid resolution of urgent issues and in launching action on a number of fronts.

The Work-Out process takes place in three distinct steps. It begins with a design phase, then the principal work is achieved in the second step, a one- to three-day event in which participants accomplish what might ordinarily take months in the normal course of business. After the event, an organized follow-up process helps make sure the accomplishments are successfully implemented.

Design

In the beginning, leaders set the performance target for the Work-Out and plan the session. Often they have help from a small design team. The design phase usually takes a few weeks, although it can happen in just a few days. Two examples:

Electrocomponents is a U.K.-based distribution company that had recently consolidated its field sales force with its telephone sales force—a major reorganization intended to revive flagging sales. One Work-Out conducted with the telephone sales group was quite successful—boosting sales by £300,000 in the hundred days. Based on this success, Nick Spetch, head of U.K. Sales, decided to use the process to accelerate the launch of new regionally focused sales units.

In a meeting of all fourteen regional and telesales managers, Spetch selected two of the new sales teams to be the focus of the next Work-Outs. He began the design process by setting aggressive goals for sales improvement in the two regions. In the next few weeks, the two sales managers and their teams held working sessions to decide on the agenda, on the work that might be done at the Work-Out event, and on a tentative participants list. The design was finalized in discussions with Spetch. Then invitations and preliminary assignments were sent out.

Leaders of the Department of Transportation for a state government in the United States decided they needed a Work-Out to begin breaking down bureaucracy and providing better service to customers. The design of this Work-Out was done in one meeting. The leadership team decided to work on improving customer service and on streamlining routine types of procedures—both projects aimed at making the department much more effective and customer-responsive. The groups included the Road Maintenance unit, the Permits Department, and the Department of Airports and Sea Ports. They selected a cross section of people to attend and set a plan for inviting them and providing them with some orientation and preliminary assignments.

The Event

The Work-Out event itself is the heart of the process. This involves from twenty to more than a hundred participants from all levels and functions in the business. It lasts between one and three days, depending on the complexity of the issue being addressed.

At the beginning of the event, the leaders challenge participants to solve an important business problem or achieve a challenging goal.

Participants then work in small teams to brainstorm ideas and to design what they believe are the best means for achieving the performance goal. They develop plans for putting these ideas into action. In a "Town Meeting" at the end of the Work-Out session, teams present their recommended plans to the leadership group and to their fellow participants. There is discussion and debate and, most important, an immediate yes-or-no decision by senior management. By the end of the Work-Out event, an agenda for action has been approved.

For example:

Over the course of both regional two-day Work-Outs, the Electrocomponents groups reviewed sales data and customer opportunities, and they developed some very specific proposals for action to improve sales in their regions. Among other things, they designed some initiatives for the telephone sales groups to help qualify leads. They also developed a plan for same-day delivery to local customers. And they established specific plans for visiting locations that had never been visited or had not been visited in several years. When the participants at both Work-Outs presented their plans at their Town Meetings, Spetch and the other assembled managers replied with an enthusiastic thumbs-up.

In the state transportation department more than forty people—from all levels, union and nonunion—participated in the Work-Out. Over the course of a full day, five groups brainstormed and then developed recommendations for reducing bureaucratic waste and delays.

One of the teams recommended a streamlined process for granting new business permits and rights of way, reducing the time by several weeks. Another team developed an innovative way to reduce road congestion and increase worker productivity by piloting new work schedules. A third team cut in half the number of steps needed to respond to customer complaints, meaning more timely responses for customers and significant labor savings for the department.

Implementation

The products of the Work-Out are always decisions that are to be implemented at once or rapid-cycle projects that must be carried out in a short time. During the implementation period, senior management holds structured review sessions. At the end, there is a formal review meeting to reflect on what has been achieved and to plan how to sustain the momentum.

Each Electrocomponents sales team held a meeting right after their Work-Out—to plan how they would work over the following three months to accomplish the results and to track and manage progress. Weekly team meetings and periodic reviews with senior sales leaders helped the team implement their plans successfully and also modify their plans based on what they learned along the way.

For example, one team originally decided to sell more electric cables to midsized and large contractors. After a few weeks they were surprised to discover that these contractors could negotiate better prices with a competitor. So they targeted small electrical contractors instead. By the end of three months, the two teams had achieved £1.1 million in additional sales—a 50 percent improvement over normal sales levels.

At the state transportation office, implementation of Work-Out-approved actions was led by the management team in each department. The commissioner of transportation conducted periodic reviews as part of his meetings with his executive team. In most cases, implementation happened within just a few weeks. The number of signatures required on key documents or on sign-offs for new permits was reduced by 50 percent, for example. One longer complex project was pilot-tested. It was a new process for performing regular roadway maintenance. The aim was to reduce traffic jams and to increase the amount of time workers were productive on the job. These pilots proved so successful that union and management agreed to write these new work rules into the next union contract so they could become the new way of working.

Successes in Work-Outs like these can lead quickly to even wider-scale efforts. In Electrocomponents the success of the first Work-Out in telephone sales led to the two Work-Outs in the regional sales teams. That yielded £1.1 million in additional revenue and it led to a "Best Practices" Work-Out. That one included people from all the sales regions, decided which of the initiatives from the two earlier Work-Outs would be rolled out more broadly, and yielded several million more pounds. It was followed by a "week of Work-Outs" with all sales personnel from the fourteen regions—about 240 people—in six major Work-Outs across the United Kingdom. The results of all this work? The first six months of pilot testing the Work-Out approach had generated almost £1.5 million incremental revenue. The expanded use of Work-Out over the next six months produced more than £6 million in additional sales revenue.

Table 5.1   Three Phases of Work-Out

1. Design	2. The Event	3. Implementation
Leaders:		
• Set overall goal	• Discuss, analyze issues	• Move into action
• Select challenge	• Brainstorm solutions	• Track progress
• Organize event	• Develop action	• Achieve results
• Conduct preliminary work	recommendation	• Build on results
	• Take decisions at Town Meeting	
	• Sharpen work plans	

In considering the possible use of Work-Out in your organization, you might consider using the following check list. Work-Out is the solution of choice when you urgently need immediate decision making and rapid implementation, and where

- The improvement opportunity cuts across different functional groups, business units, branches, or regions.
- The improvement opportunity is somewhat complex, and root causes and solutions are not immediately obvious.
- Input is needed from a large number of diverse groups of people to identify possible solutions.

On the other hand, Work-Out will not achieve much for you when any of the following factors are at work:

- The main objective is to get buy-in of participants to decisions that have already been made.
- Management is not prepared to make immediate decisions and launch immediate action.
- The objective is a reduction of staff.

Eagle Star Insurance Turns to Work-Out

In the late 1990s, one-hundred-year-old Eagle Star Insurance was in serious difficulty. The company was the third largest general insurance firm in the United Kingdom. But, mainly as a result of striving for market share at almost any cost, its losses were great. When Patrick O'Sullivan entered the scene he was the company's sixth chief executive in as many years. Within a few weeks it became apparent to him that many of the company's managers were in denial about the difficult situation. And to complicate his task, two months into his new job, it was announced that the company was being merged into Zurich Financial Services in what would be a long and involved process.

O'Sullivan gathered a few senior executives and made it clear that action was needed to stem their losses very quickly. At the same time they would have to conduct a major strategy review to decide where the company should be headed.

It was easy to identify the most urgent performance improvement goals that had to be attacked at once. Claims leakage at that moment— payments in excess of the amount that well-managed claims would require—was running about 10-20 percent. With the equivalent of more than a billion U.S. dollars in claims payments each year, these overpayments were an obvious early target. Moreover, the lengthy delays and poor claims service were driving customers into the arms of competitors.

Work-Out Generates Rapid Involvement and Rapid Results

O'Sullivan led the first Work-Out aimed at improving Claims Department performance. He convened more than fifty staff members from both of the company's major business divisions (personal and commercial), representing more than a dozen local branches, with the goal of saving more than $10 million in claims payments that year. The twenty-plus senior managers—to whom the Work-Out participants reported— participated in the Town Meeting session where the final decisions were taken. They were later involved as sponsors of the improvement efforts that they approved in the Town Meeting.

Though it seemed a very ambitious target, the participants were able to develop more than a dozen major improvement recommendations. Action plans to implement those ideas were quickly approved by senior management at the end of the session. Some were simple ideas such as a plan to collect more of the millions of dollars in claims reimbursements legitimately due to the company. Others were more complex, such as revamping the company's network of automobile repair shops, and helping the dozens of claims representatives across the company do more to manage costs.

These ideas were quickly assigned to teams working within and across branches and involving dozens of other people across all of the Claims operations. And the results began occurring quickly. As the first hundred days of rapid-cycle efforts ended, a number of branches began holding a second round of smaller-scale Work-Outs to expand on their efforts. Some branches collaborated with other locations to share and build on best practices. By the end of the first six months, several hundred claims staff were actively engaged in a variety of improvement projects. For most of them it was the first time they had worked that way. And for their managers, it was the first time they had to manage such autonomous and energized subordinates.

CEO O'Sullivan fashioned his first meeting of the leadership group of the newly merged company as a major Work-Out—involving all 150 of the company's top managers. Over the course of two days, small teams addressed the areas that formed the core of the company's strategic "back to basics" focus—areas such as underwriting and pricing, expense control and financial management, and, of course, claims processing. By enlisting them as Work-Out participants, the aim was to help these leaders—many of whom were skeptical about the value of wide-scale involvement—experience the power of this approach, while at the same time driving home the message that they had to produce significant improvements in results, and do so quickly. Shortly after this leadership Work-Out a number of managers took the plunge and held their own Work-Outs to address performance improvement issues in their parts of the company.

As we describe in Chapter Six, within a few years tens of millions in savings were achieved, and thousands of people across the company were involved through Work-Outs—with many more also involved in post–Work-Out implementation efforts. A new focus on frontline involvement, management decision making, and accountability for rapid action and results had taken hold throughout the company—contributing to a major financial turnaround and the resurgence of the organization.

Work-Out at Armstrong

At Zurich U.K., the process of wide-scale involvement took several years to roll out across the company. At Avery Dennison, a global roll-out took just a year. In the case of Armstrong Industries, wide-scale involvement reached across the company in just a few months.

Armstrong is a $3 billion global company that manufactures flooring materials, ceiling tiles, and cabinets for kitchens and bathrooms. In early 2001, despite recent successes and good growth prospects, the company was facing major performance challenges. Most significant was the threat of asbestos liability and with it the prospect of fundamental financial restructuring. Mike Lockhart, the new CEO, was faced with the need to demonstrate rapid performance improvement and cultural change to the investment community and other stakeholders.

Lockhart had formerly worked at GE and had experienced the power of Work-Out. He therefore decided to introduce a process similar to Work-Out, to be called "Trailblazing," as the primary vehicle for change. Within a matter of weeks the Customer Service Department of Armstrong Flooring Products Division was selected for the first Trailblazing session. The department was not performing at the desired level; its people were quoting incorrect prices, making errors in bills, and not providing good service when dealing with claims. The focus for this first Trailblazing was "Making Customer Service a Competitive Advantage."

Mike Lockhart and the head of the Flooring Products Division were to provide overall guidance while two other managers would provide the active leadership of the work. Because of the urgency, this initial Trailblazing session to involve about sixty people was designed in one day. Four teams were created, with each team to focus on one topic. A specific goal was set for each, to be achieved in about twelve weeks. (See Table 5.2.)

In addition to its goal, each team was given a set of thought-starter questions. Here, for example, are two of the Pricing/Billing team's questions:

- What could be done to ensure Customer Service Reps (CSRs) always have the correct prices for new products?
- What could be done to ensure CSRs are aware of all the special price lists?

The Trailblazing session lasted two and a half days. After introductions by the senior managers who had planned the session and an overview

Table 5.2   Armstrong Projects

Team	Goal
Pricing/Billing Team	Quote accurate prices to customers in all cases on the first request, and eliminate billing errors due to incorrect prices.
Product and Promotion Information Team	Satisfactorily answer on the first call all requests for information on new and dropped products and special promotions, beginning with product changes and promotions, in April 2001.
Claims Resolution Team	Resolve 95 percent of claims within thirty days of receipt of the complaint.
Claims Prevention Team	Reduce the average number of weekly complaints by 30 percent.

of the Trailblazing methodology by the consultant helping to run the process, the four teams got to work. Each team had to agree on the top ten ideas that had the best chance of achieving its goal. For example, the Pricing/Billing team determined that pricing misquotes and billing errors were caused in part by the fact that the pricing data was located in too many different places. Thus the data was not easy to access and was often inaccurate. The team decided to create a single, easy-to-access electronic pricing database for all Armstrong personnel to use. This change in itself was expected to reduce errors by 30 percent. Each of the teams developed many such ideas.

The teams presented their top ten ideas at the Town Meeting on the last afternoon. Mike Lockhart and the division general manager made yes-or-no decisions on the spot. The vast majority of ideas were approved.

The next day the four team leaders and a few key members from each of the teams met for a full-day Implementation Workshop to detail the work plans, specify responsibilities, and agree on tracking mechanisms. During the implementation process they had weekly team meetings as well as informal review sessions between team leaders and champions. There were formal reviews at thirty and sixty days.

At the end of the ninety-day Trailblazing period, the Sponsors held a formal closure meeting with the teams to review results achieved and to lay out plans for the next phase. All four teams had successfully met—and beaten—their goals.

While the four initial teams were at work, the company's Operating Committee had begun to plan the process of rolling out Trailblazing across the company. Twenty internal facilitators were trained to support the process in their own units.

Immediately after the completion of the first four projects, a second Trailblazing was launched in Armstrong Building Products, and a third one was scheduled for Armstrong Wood Products to begin within a month.

Mike Lockhart insisted that all major divisions adopt Trailblazing. So, within a few months, Trailblazing was blazing all over Armstrong. During the first year fourteen Trailblazing events were held. In the second year a hundred Trailblazing events were held across the world, facilitated by seventy-five trained internal consultants. More than a thousand people were involved in generating $30 million in savings.

Change as Fast as You Want to Make It Happen

There is a paradoxical lesson to be learned from the experiences of Avery Dennison, Zurich U.K., and Armstrong cited in this chapter. Rapid-cycle projects, even if somewhat modest to begin with, can quickly be turned into powerful engines for accelerating change—change that can advance as fast as you want it to happen and can involve huge numbers of people as quickly as you want to involve them. Elaborate culture-change programs, on the other hand, with huge up-front investments of energy and resources, rarely accomplish nearly as much—and often fail to accomplish anything of value.

As more and more people lead and participate in rapid results teams, more and more change management competence is developed at every level in the organization. And as this competence grows, so does the organization's overall capacity to implement

large-scale change. Chapter Six describes how senior management can exploit this rapidly expanding capacity by designing an
architecture of change that is uniquely suited to what it is trying
to achieve.

Key Points

- Major change requires mobilization of large numbers of
  people—not just the same old reliables.

- Initial rapid results projects may be modest in scope,
  but many can then be launched quickly.

- A few pilot breakthroughs set the pattern for the rest.

- Large numbers of people and functions can be involved
  rapidly.

- The GE Work-Out can be used for mobilizing large numbers of people in rapid-cycle change—quickly.

6

BUILD YOUR OWN UNIQUE TRANSFORMATION PROCESS

Of all the CEOs who will be tossing and turning tonight, you can bet that a large number of them will be wondering how to carry out some kind of major transformations in their companies: reversing profit deterioration, adapting to radical marketplace shifts, accelerating slow growth, quickening the pace of innovation.

Armies of consultants and academics have invested major effort in trying to create the right formula for executing these transformations, but without much success. Although some of the models have won many converts and acolytes, none has really demonstrated lasting value.

The weakness of master models was demonstrated by the landmark Harvard Business School study conducted by Michael Beer and his colleagues, mentioned in Chapter One. After studying a number of attempted major transformations in a variety of corporations, the researchers concluded that company-wide change efforts based on formally structured programs failed to achieve their aims. As they colorfully put it, "Wave after wave of programs rolled across the landscape with little positive impact."[1] By contrast, the successful efforts tended to be empirically developed by the companies themselves. And in those companies the change process emanated not from top down but from bottom up.

Our own observations of many attempted transformations strongly suggest that no universal change template has yet been

---

This chapter is based on the article "Build Your Own Change Model," *Business Horizons*, May-June 2004, by Robert H. Schaffer and Matthew K. McCreight.

discovered—nor is any waiting to be discovered. While organizations can certainly benefit from the cumulative experience of others, we are convinced that each organization must create a unique change process that works best for itself. In this chapter we sketch a framework by which management teams can carry out the experimentation and learning necessary to accomplish that process. It is not a change architecture in itself but rather a framework that enables each organization to construct its own change architecture.

A Radical Departure: Design Each Organization's Transition Process as a Unique Creative Work

The basic idea we advance in this chapter is that a major transformational change effort should be divided into a series of discrete staged advances, each about four to six months long, each focused on a set of agreed-upon overall objectives, and each with a clear beginning and a clear end.

Within each of these stages, a number of planned change steps are carried out. From the beginning, rapid results projects provide much of the energy and drive. And each rapid results project is designed to produce urgently needed business results that will move the organization toward its transformational goals for that period—while, in addition and at the same time yielding some new managerial capability in implementing change and some new insights about the corporation's strategy.

The successes during each stage provide the zest and confidence for moving ahead. And at the end of each phase, the achievements and associated learning are assessed, and the resulting wisdom is exploited in the design of the subsequent period. Thus the number of projects as well as their individual scope can expand in each successive stage.

Since the idea is to create an integrated transformation strategy that knits together all the changing elements, there needs to be a group at the top to manage and coordinate the effort. We suggest that the chief executive officer and a group of senior managers form themselves into a change steering committee (which you will undoubtedly want to give a more dramatic name). Their job will be to orchestrate the creation and execution of the overall change process. This is not a one-shot task. They should consider that this responsibility adds a major new dimension to their jobs, and they should regard the creation of a change process for their organization as a task that will require constant adjustment, modification, and renewal.

Learning to carry out that task is a major developmental experience for the senior group.

Strategic Plans Drive Rapid Results Projects; Rapid Results Projects Inform Strategic Planning

When the change steering committee (or whatever you choose to call it) convenes, its first job is to agree as rapidly as possible on two points:

- The members' current view of where they want to be in a few years—that is, the agreed-upon strategic goals for the organization.
- Within that framework, the most urgent performance improvement and change goals—that is, what they need to attack immediately to begin pursuing the strategic goals.

To initiate progress toward each of those urgent change goals, they should charge certain managers with the responsibility of launching rapid-cycle, results-focused projects.

As noted, these rapid-cycle projects must be designed both to achieve important business goals and to advance the key strategic objectives. Since these projects will help to develop implementation capability where they are carried out, it is important to get action under way fairly quickly. Then, while successful work on the projects goes forward, helping to generate an upbeat feeling throughout the organization, senior management can continue to examine and refine the overall strategic plans.

While all this is getting under way, it is important to share the nature of the process and how it is working with the entire organization—with the clear message that everyone will shortly be engaged in moving the process forward.

Many purists will be affronted by the idea of initiating change projects before a comprehensive strategic change plan is set in concrete. They assert that these rapid results projects could "lead the company in the wrong direction." But that's a fantasy. These initial projects are designed to yield urgently needed results quickly—without major investment and in ways that do not commit the organization to any fundamental strategic shifts, so there is no such risk. The projects, of course, need to cohere with the existing corporate strategy just as the strategic plans need to be influenced by what is being learned about the organization's implementation capability. Chapter Ten details this symbiosis between strategic planning and rapid results, elaborating on the concept that planning and implementation are the chicken-and-egg of corporate transformation—they should proceed in parallel, each nourishing the other.

Zurich U.K.—A Case in Point

In Chapter Five, we recounted the experience of the Zurich U.K. insurance company. When it was still called Eagle Star Insurance, a new CEO, Patrick O'Sullivan, had been brought in to turn the company around. Before doing anything else, he had to stem the company's disastrous losses. As described in Chapter Five, he focused first on the Claims Department, where payments were estimated to be running at 10–20 percent over what they should have been—in a situation in which claims were over a billion dollars a year. In several Work-Out sessions, O'Sullivan quickly began to plug up the claims leakage.

Other similar rapid-cycle cost-reduction projects were launched in other areas of the business during the first six months, most of them via Work-Out sessions similar to the claims session. The leadership team initiated its own efforts to terminate activities that were not really essential, thus modeling such initiatives for the rest of the organization. They found many ways to put the brakes on the spending momentum. Certain marketing expenses, for example, were cut, and IT projects that at the time were running millions over budget were brought under greater control.

Rapid-Cycle Projects Develop Implementation Capacity and Create Confidence and Enthusiasm

Rapid-cycle projects, by generating tangible success, reinforce senior management's message that the organization must do better and, moreover, that it has the capacity to do so. The successes help people overcome their self-doubts as they see the evidence that they can indeed achieve more. Before Eagle Star became Zurich U.K. denial had served as a defense against taking action. Rapid results were crucial to changing the psychological climate.

Beyond achieving needed results, these projects serve as building blocks of the total change process and are carried out as learning experiences. Here are some examples of the developmental ingredients that were deliberately designed into the projects done by Zurich U.K.

Go for Results at Once. By demonstrating that the organization has the capacity to produce tangible results at once, rapid-cycle projects overcome the frequent tendency to begin change efforts with endless preparations and studies. That is why it is important to carve out goals that participants feel reasonably certain they can achieve.

The first Claims project in the company succeeded in eliminating several million dollars in claims costs (even though it fell somewhat short of its ambitious $10 million savings goal). It also gave participants the confidence that they could do much more. A series of rapid-cycle projects were then launched in key branches to expand on the first claims improvements. For example, one major branch—with more than 150 claims handlers—focused on helping each claims representative work to reduce overpayments, and savings quickly totaled more than $100,000 a month. It also instilled a new sense of pride among these claims representatives.

The Finance group tackled ways to improve cash flow. With the goal of a $30 million improvement in cash flow in two months, they launched a series of rapid results projects. By making some immediate changes in financing strategy the team exceeded their goal and added more than $2 million to the company's bottom line within a few weeks. When asked why the change had not been carried out previously, a member of the frontline Finance group sighed, "No one would have listened."

No amount of planning or training or new systems can provide the zest and reinforcement yielded by the achievement of rapid results like these. At Zurich U.K. they reinforced O'Sullivan's determination to push for ever-more-rapid progress. Success began to dissolve the web of denial the staff had woven around themselves.

Managerial Skill Development. The rapid development of new skills and capabilities among managers is crucial to the success of any transformation. Rapid results projects are designed as learning laboratories to help managers expand their capabilities in managing change. Modifying their management styles, instituting new ways to sponsor and support change efforts, reorienting processes and metrics to focus on crucial goals—and more—can all be deliberately built into such projects.

At Zurich U.K., the rapid-cycle projects were designed with a deliberate developmental agenda for managers. As projects were defined, accountable managers were named. They participated in just-in-time training and coaching sessions to develop the skills they would need to sponsor the projects. As part of the push to accelerate the pace, small groups of manager-level people were trained to serve as internal consultants. Under the leadership of Organization Development Director Mo Kang, these internal consultants helped an increasing number of managers become involved and build their own skills in the process.

Introduction of New Tools and Business Processes. The rapid-cycle projects can be used to test new ways of getting things done. These include streamlining business processes, partnering with customers, managing inventory, and developing new products. These and dozens of other processes can all be advanced—as can new elements of information technology, new budgeting processes, new measurement and management information schemes, and other disciplines that are needed to drive constantly improving organizational performance.

When the first projects in Claims were under way, the internal consulting team began issuing monthly updates of the results being achieved. The initial reaction was one of anger. As Mo Kang put it: "When we issued the first update on the results being achieved by the various work teams, it revealed that a number of teams were not yet making any progress. I received a number of angry calls over the next few days. 'How dare you publish that kind of stuff.' But Patrick [O'Sullivan] pushed right back and told the whole company that this sort of update would be done every month. People got the message pretty quickly that results mattered."

CEO Patrick O'Sullivan and CFO Bryan Howett then initiated a series of monthly operating reviews where each business unit leader and team had to report on current business achievements. They also had to state the actions they each would take to close any gaps in performance against plan.

Advance Strategic Thrusts. The rapid-cycle projects can be used to test and advance important strategic thrusts such as launching new products, venturing into new markets, and integrating acquisitions.

These pilot efforts reduce the "bet your company" feeling associated with many major strategic moves. For example, the initial rapid-cycle projects in Claims provided the basic data needed for a far-reaching strategic transformation of the entire Claims organization to further reduce claims overpayments.

Rather than attacking this transformation on a big-fix, company-wide basis, Roger Day, head of Claims, formed a small team of representatives from various offices who made a quick survey in just one part of the business. The large claims losses they found—and the improvements they were able to quickly effect—validated the fundamental changes they were proposing, even to the most skeptical claims managers. Similar reviews were then held throughout the business, with similar benefits.

These strategic reviews highlighted the need to reorganize the five major Claims branches in the Commercial Division. Effective control of claims costs would require much more uniformity and discipline among offices. Claims leader Geoff McMahon asked a cross-functional team to get the new processes designed and put in place in all offices in just four months, and they succeeded. This was one of many examples of how the company's strategy began to be shaped from the bottom up as well as the top down.

Another strategic drive that was advanced with rapid-cycle projects was the process of integrating Eagle Star into the global Zurich organization. One Work-Out session, with both Zurich corporate and Eagle Star people, was held to plan the integration. By the end of the few days, they had planned out how to do it and they had also launched a number of actions that would quickly save hundreds of thousands of dollars. Just as important, they had started to build a common organization. In the words of one participant, "We started as two separate groups. Now, just a few days later, I feel like we are now one company."

Thus did Zurich U.K. begin to create its own transformation process. Rapid results projects were the core. Management skill development was designed into the projects. New tools and new business procedures were introduced to facilitate progress and strengthen the infrastructure. And as new insights emerged about strategic directions, they guided the selection of subsequent waves of action projects.

End of Each Cycle: What Are We Learning? What Should We Accomplish in the Next Cycle?

Michael Beer and his team advise that "change is about learning." This simple but profound concept is at the heart of the build-your-own process that we are advocating. As each four- to six-month cycle is completed, senior management can assess what was achieved in that cycle and what can be learned from the experiences. As part of these reviews, the steering committee might meet with the sponsors of all the projects to get some details of what was accomplished, what was learned, and what possible implications for next steps are emerging.

They need to see whether modifications need to be made in the longer-term strategic outlook. They can then decide what needs be accomplished in the next stage.

The managers leading projects need to make deliberate choices about what will be built into projects in the way of managerial and methodological innovations. And, when the project plans are written, they must include not only a description of the project and its goal but also a description of what innovations are to be tested and how their effectiveness will be assessed—and how their project will be contributing to progress toward the strategic goals.

Each organization has to test the cycle time that is best for it. Four to six months has proven to be about right for most organizations, but some prefer shorter cycles in the early stages. A one-year cycle, even though it matches many other scheduled events in an organization's life, is usually too long until the achievement and learning cycle is sufficiently embedded.

At the very beginning of the process, the cycle of achievement, learning, and planning should probably be initiated and led by the senior-level steering committee. Once under way, the process can be diffused. Different units of the organization might create their own steering committees to support and manage the change efforts within their own spheres. And, where useful, other steering groups might be established on a pro tem basis to manage certain key change initiatives.

Gradually the change process becomes an organization-wide shared experimentation and learning experience, with an increasing number of rapid-cycle projects of increasing scope being carried out in each phase of the change process—and, withal, reflecting the unique character of the organization and its people.

Strategic Planning Is Continuous

In the traditional view of corporate transformations, it is an article of faith that strategic planning must be the first step of any major transformation. But this is an intellectually specious construction. It is based on the fantasy that sufficiently diligent up-front work will permit strategic planners to map out a change process in advance. That ignores four major risks in strategic planning:

- *Implementation shortfall:* The risk that a number of the planned implementation steps will not be carried out as planned and therefore will not contribute their expected momentum to the overall change.
- *White space:* The risk that a number of necessary activities will not be anticipated or planned for.
- *Integration failure:* The risk that the various strands of strategic activity may not come together in mutually integrative ways.
- *Unanticipated shifts:* The risk that events within the organization or in the outside world will disrupt the chain of assumptions on which the strategic plans are based.

In the conventional mode any of these occurrences is a torpedo into the hull of the strategic plan. In the process we advocate, these risks are mostly eliminated because strategic plans are considered to be working documents—good for today, but modifiable tomorrow with fresh experience. That is why the strategic planning process and the implementation process must advance simultaneously—each providing fresh insights and lessons for the other on a continuing basis.

For example, at Zurich U.K., as bottom-line results improved, the strategic focus shifted from stemming losses to expanding profits. The leadership team met early in 2000 and charted a course to move ahead of the competition in terms of cost levels. This required them to beat the already-challenging profit targets they had just set for themselves. A few years earlier, a large consulting firm had presented them with a set of ambitious strategic plans quite oblivious to the fact that the company had no energy or capability to implement them. By this time, however, with the confidence and competence bred of the dozens of successful rapid results projects, they knew they could accomplish their goals.

While an increasing number of rapid results projects are being carried out, those responsible for overall strategic planning keep the process going. The rapid-cycle projects are always selected to best advance the strategic plans (as they exist at the time). And the influence travels the other way also: as the rapid results projects yield results and provide new experience, those lessons are deliberately factored into the ongoing strategic planning process.

In Chapter Ten, we address in more detail this critical linkage between immediate action and strategic planning.

Institutional Modifications to Support the Change Process

As the results-focused action projects and the strategic innovations create momentum and confidence, the steering committee can begin to design and implement the major institutional changes that will cement the progress to date and advance the process going forward:

- Organization structure changes
- Staffing of key positions
- Capital investment and modes of financing
- Information and decision systems
- New compensation practices
- Major process redesign
- Technology and information systems

Many organizations make changes in these institutional elements at the beginning of a transformation process, hoping to generate momentum. But that puts the cart before the horse: institutional changes can reinforce momentum already created, but can rarely generate it.

As noted earlier, at Zurich U.K., one early innovation was the formation of a central internal consulting group of about six people to champion the company's change process and help instill a results focus into its change efforts. This group trained the two-hundred-plus members of the management team and more than three hundred other employees (almost 10 percent of the workforce) in various change leadership and change facilitation skills and roles. This training was results-oriented and conducted within the context of the ongoing rapid-cycle projects.

The company's management conferences—which formerly had been largely set piece events focused mostly on speeches and socializing—became "change acceleration events." The first conference of the top 150 managers after the announcement of the merger between Eagle Star and Zurich was a two-day event where teams developed plans for achieving an additional $15 million in savings—above the amount already budgeted. At the conference a series of additional rapid results projects were launched in underwriting, pricing, claims, and cost management.

Subsequent management conferences launched other rapid results efforts under this new strategic banner. For example, one conference focused on innovation; it launched a series of new business ventures—

all of which had to be developed and tested within a few months. Success on these new business thrusts led to a more ongoing boundaryless
attack on innovation—with a cross-business innovation council meeting
regularly to review ideas, sponsor projects, and agree on funding for
proven ideas.

At the end of four-plus years Zurich U.K. was a very different
company from the old Eagle Star. It had shifted earnings from a significant loss to strong and sustained profits. It had improved the
bottom line by more than $100 million a year (as verified by the
company's actuaries) and, according to CEO O'Sullivan, it had
benefited by multiples of that amount in additional benefits that
could not be clearly measured. Moreover, it was a different company, moving into new markets and experimenting with new products and new ways of doing business. Instead of the old inertia,
constant change had become a routine and not a battle.

The rapid results projects, accelerating and expanding, achieved
the bottom-line results. At the same time they helped to introduce the many new skills and tools essential for continued performance gains. While Zurich U.K. was driving dozens of rapid-cycle
improvement projects, senior management was constantly analyzing what they were learning and how to move it forward.

Although they exploited the GE Work-Out process and some
other specific change techniques in mobilizing action, the overall
change process was their own creation. It was a process over which
they labored long and one that evolved and changed over time,
nourished by a steady stream of positive results.

Master of Your Fate—Not Victim of Circumstance

If you want a high-success approach to transforming your organization you need follow only one aspect of the Zurich U.K. model:
create an orderly way to launch the various elements of your developmental process and work hard at learning from success. As you

create your own transformation process, you will increasingly become master of your fate—rather than a victim of your circumstances. You will undoubtedly use tools and processes that differ from Zurich U.K.'s, but you can accomplish the same success.

In Chapter Seven we show how Georgia-Pacific exploited rapid results projects to achieve huge financial dividends as well as the other developmental benefits that rapid-cycle success can provide. Then Part Three will provide insights into how rapid-cycle projects can serve as the building blocks of major transformations.

Key Points

- Searching for the perfect change model that your company can follow is a waste of energy.
- Each company is unique and must create its unique change architecture.
- A quick sketch of the company's strategy provides the context and direction for change—the compass that is essential when getting started.
- Rapid results projects then quickly create momentum to move toward the strategic direction—along with learning, confidence, and data for further planning.
- Strategy and action then evolve together in four- to six-month waves of change.
- As the process progresses, other internal and external supporting changes evolve in concert.

7

GEORGIA-PACIFIC
TAKES IT ALL THE WAY

The essential message of this book is that rapid-cycle projects not only yield immediate and rewarding gains but also can serve as the foundation for far-reaching transformations. Georgia-Pacific of Atlanta, Georgia, a $20 billion corporation with fifty-five thousand employees, has demonstrated how that occurs.

After ten years of using rapid-cycle improvement, this implementation process is in place throughout the company. It is the engine that drives continuous improvement not only at the plant level but also throughout the business. In their Consumer Products facilities alone, in 2002, $300 million a year of sustained cost reduction and cost-impacting productivity gains were documented and audited—and in 2003 another $300 million of improvement was achieved.

Georgia-Pacific Consumer Products is a vertically integrated set of businesses that manufacture a variety of paper towels, toilet paper, Dixie cups, and plates and napkins. The company also makes consumer brands of copy and printer papers, as well as packaging and a wide range of building products. Wal-Mart is the company's biggest consumer products customer.

The process started small and grew rapidly. It has driven major profit improvement and has been a major implementation tool in the rapid growth of the corporation through acquisition. As described in Chapter Six, the process is also used to drive broad business improvement and to feed strategy, with teams at both the business and corporate levels tackling difficult management resource allocation issues and system improvements. It has helped turn around a noncompetitive mill with corrosive union relationships. It has achieved major gains in the management of logistics.

How It Began

A. D. (Pete) Correll provided the impetus for the process in the paper mills when he became CEO of Georgia-Pacific in 1993. He decentralized manufacturing management for the paper mills and directed that a facility-based strategy be developed for each mill. A pilot diagnostic effort was launched at two facilities (Port Hudson, Louisiana, and Cedar Springs, Georgia).

A team from each mill worked with a team of consultants to define gaps for cost or productivity improvement. A team of internal consultants was assembled to help drive the effort. The entire workforce at those mills was engaged in idea generation, and every idea was documented.

As the diagnostic efforts proceeded with these full-time teams, uneasiness grew at the corporate level. The teams were identifying lots of opportunities for improvement, but there was no obvious methodology to ensure implementation. Correll and Charles E. Hodges (who headed the internal team) encountered the idea of rapid-cycle projects and decided to use such projects as the core method for achieving results. The method was tested in the two pilot mills.

The process was extraordinarily successful. Hodges expanded his group, and two more mills volunteered to be next. By the time the process was established at those two mills in 1995, the methodology was fully structured as the Mill Improvement Process, and teams of internal MIP specialists were created. Four specialist teams were set up to work with the fine-paper mills, pulp mills, and containerboard mills. A separate effort was also initiated to work with the corrugated box plants. The corporate steering committee led by Correll continued to lead the process. The MIP specialist group headed by Hodges was assimilated into the corporate

Engineering Department. The vice president of engineering provided sponsorship and conveyed the idea that the process was going to be a continuing effort rather than a short-term improvement program.

At each new mill, the MIP specialist team would do some preliminary diagnostic work on-site with the mill manager and controller, help to name a mill process leader (usually a full-time position), and help mill leadership identify a steering committee (usually the mill manager's direct reports) and a diagnostic team. The members of the diagnostic team were generally department heads or leaders and were taken off their regular jobs for the ten weeks of the diagnostic. The MIP specialist group facilitated the diagnostic work at each mill and helped the steering committee master its leadership role.

How the Mill Improvement Process Works

Over the next few years, the rapid results process was adapted to Georgia-Pacific's unique requirements. A highly structured ten-week process was designed, and it is directed in each mill by its steering committee. Unlike most of the other cases cited in earlier chapters, this process begins with a formal diagnostic step. Of all the ideas generated in the diagnosis, the few that seem to offer the greatest returns are selected by a senior sponsor and a designated team leader. With the help of a staff breakthrough specialist each team leader conducts an all-day kickoff meeting of the cross-functional team to set a "razor sharp goal," establish measurement and tracking methods, and develop a work plan to achieve the goal within six weeks—less than fifty days!

At the end of two weeks each team holds a formal review with the mill steering committee to review the goal and early progress achieved. At the six-week point there is another review since each team is expected to have implemented their work plan and reached their goal. At this six-week review, teams shift their attention to the sustainability of their improvement (while they continue to work on implementing the ongoing improvement).

At ten weeks, the teams present their final review. It focuses on the detailed sustainability plans each team has developed. One team member—usually the leader—assumes responsibility for continuing to track results.

The process advances in each mill as a series of ten-week waves. At the beginning of each wave eight to fifteen projects are launched simultaneously. Then, ten weeks later, as the projects in each wave are winding down, the next wave is gearing up.

Evolution of the Mill Improvement Process

The Mill Improvement Process was implemented on a mill-by-mill basis. Each facility was expected to run the process with a very high degree of independence—even calling the process by a unique local name. (This philosophy has carried forward to the present as the process was extended to new units.)

Recognition and rewards centered on these independent identities, with each mill process having its own name and logo that appears on a wide variety of T-shirts, golf shirts, jackets, and ball caps—most given for successful completion of diagnostic or team efforts. While the core diagnostic and improvement wave process was very highly structured and consistently applied, a great deal of independence was fostered in dealing with sponsorship, communication, and team selection issues. Each mill developed a very high sense of ownership in its process.

By 1997, all the major facilities in the corporation had a MIP going, each led by the facility's manager and a steering team. Each had developed an independent culture and name, but all were consistent in how the methodology was used to get rapid-cycle improvement in ten weeks. While the diagnostic process engaged the entire workforce in the generation of ideas, the implementation waves at that time were still primarily a management process in the paper mills.

Expanding the Involvement of People

The next mill in line for the MIP was a small recycled paper mill in Kalamazoo then managed by Rick Larrick. He was very concerned about the resource drain that the intense MIP implementation would require. To deal with that, Larrick reached out further into the organization to recruit MIP participants. The local union president was brought onto the mill steering committee and offered a leadership role in identifying improvement issues and leading change. The steering committee included production workers to staff the ten-week diagnostic team. While information had always been openly shared at the plant, this diagnostic team had access to the books and to any other information they needed to do their work. Ideas were generated as in the other plants, but this time ownership of the ideas was much more widespread among the workforce. As the implementation progressed to the first improvement waves, great enthusiasm built up in the workforce. The breakthrough teams included significant numbers of production workers. By the second wave, several teams were led by production workers.

In 1999, Larrick took over the corporate MIP leadership role. Most of the mills had introduced the process, and the corporate group of MIP specialists shifted focus to what became known as "10-K" checkups. These were audits by corporate staff of how the process was being sustained in each mill. These corporate specialists also assisted in mills where the process was floundering.

Larrick says, "Paper mills have a tradition of strong silo organization. By making the diagnostics cross-functional, major opportunities were most often found across departmental silos. And these newer diagnostic efforts began to engage groups that were not involved in the original projects. For example, including the procurement function helped the mill to get at the true costs of yield and usage of wood, which is our biggest raw material."

An illustration of how the silo boundaries were being broken was provided by Tom Fowler, director of the Lehigh Valley Dixie Plant. In one part of his plant they package paper cups and plastic lids together. A team studied the possibility of purchasing some new equipment that could do the job more efficiently. As Fowler described it, "They found that the idea was excellent. The trouble was that the payback on the investment was not adequate. At the same time another team investigating a similar operation in the plant was about to kill their project for almost exactly the same reason. In the past, the two projects would each have been quietly buried. But because our teams are multilevel and interfunctional, the teams found out about each other's work. They got together and discovered quickly that a single investment for both uses would pay off very quickly."

Five-Year Review:
Great Progress but Opportunities to Improve

The first five years produced tremendous progress and huge savings. Senior management was gratified by what had been accomplished. Nevertheless, they identified three major issues that were drags on the program's benefits:

- In every start-up thus far mill operations had suffered significantly, generally during the second wave as mill leadership became so focused on improvement that day-to-day performance faltered. And when management attempted to compensate by focusing more on day-to-day performance the effectiveness of their MIP diminished.
- The corporate MIP specialists appeared to have become too focused on the MIP process itself and on idea generation and were losing the focus on results.
- There was little collaboration between mills. In fact, a few mills began to develop variations on the process that were taking them off in incompatible directions.

Of the three issues, the easiest to address was the focus on results. Corporate staff started "rolling up" all the claimed sustainable savings from the mills and publishing mills' results throughout the organization. The expectation for results intensified. The focus of the "10-K" audits now was even more sharply on the results achieved.

The issue of balance between ongoing operations and improvement was more difficult. In the kickoff training the need to maintain this balance was emphasized; nevertheless on almost every engagement day-to-day operations began to suffer about the middle of the second wave. In examining what had happened at the Kalamazoo Mill, Larrick observed that the people selected for the various MIP roles in the first few waves tended to be the same individuals. With the same group of people attempting to focus on so many different improvement tasks, it was not surprising that while the breakthrough projects succeeded, the operations suffered. This same pattern was confirmed at other mills.

Balancing Resources: The Plattsburgh Plant Tries a New Tack

The next start-up was the paper mill in Plattsburgh, New York. To experiment with better resource balancing, some simple changes were tested here. First, the steering committee members were not assigned any other role in MIP. Second, no leader or breakthrough specialist would have that role in more than two of any successive three improvement waves. And third, no more than 50 percent of the participants in the diagnostic phase would be assigned to wave teams in the first wave—and that 50 percent rule should always be used in planning every subsequent improvement wave. This last decision overcame the tendency of most mills to use the same team leaders and members repeatedly. These rules are not rigidly applied, but have been generally followed since that time. The increased involvement of nonsupervisory employees has also helped with resource balancing.

Creating a Collaborative Network Across the Company

The MIP had overcome the silo effect within each mill, but some initiatives were needed to overcome the silo effect between mills. Beginning in 1999 and continuing for the next few years, a series of

MIP Leadership Conferences were held at six-month intervals. Here, the process coordinators from each of the mills met for several days with corporate leadership. Mills shared the highlights of their success stories, and some process training was provided. At the first few of these conferences the major learning for most participants was that there was indeed a common improvement process across the corporation. In addition to the face-to-face leadership conferences, a series of telephone conference calls was also initiated so people could share successes and issues—and tabulate results—every two weeks.

As mill coordinators were exposed to the best practices of their counterparts, it led to a demand for more standardized tools. Training materials were shared, and consistency of the process was enhanced with common standards for the launch procedure and the two-, six- and ten-week reviews. Common communications and control tools were developed, the most notable being a common Microsoft Access idea database that aided classification of ideas by type and value. Facilities began to use study teams to break down complex improvement opportunities into quantified initiatives that could be handled by future teams.

The collaboration also led to an expanded use of benchmarking. In the initial diagnostics, most benchmarking was against a mill's own internal performance—such as the best demonstrated week. Now, with the increased collaboration, mills wanted to benchmark against each other. There was also a reinvigoration of new ideas as mill coordinators shared success stories with their counterparts and then brought the new ideas back to their own mill steering committees.

The semiannual MIP Leadership Conferences became an important tool for bringing new mills into the improvement process. Attending these conferences, the managers of newly acquired mills were exposed to a proven process that was clearly working and that was obviously not just a program-of-the-month. As the senior managers of these new facilities got ready to launch the process in their mills, they sent potential steering committee members to the conferences to learn what had been achieved at other mills.

As Charlie Hodges put it, "Georgia-Pacific was assembled mostly through acquisitions. The Mill Improvement Process introduced a common approach for the first time—where people used the same language and shared a common process."

In recent years, "lean manufacturing" and the Toyota manufacturing system have influenced the processes for both facility-level and business-level diagnostics. For example, a "value stream mapping" approach is being used in manufacturing and in administrative processes. But whatever the diagnostic methodology used to identify the opportunities, the MIP rapid-cycle project strategy is applied to drive the results.

MIP Brings Synergy to Life

Near the end of 2000, Georgia-Pacific acquired the Fort James Corporation. This more than doubled the tissue paper capacity and the number of facilities. Georgia-Pacific had promised the investment community significant synergistic improvement from the merger. These benefits were generated by establishing "synergy teams" in each functional area to find and drive commonality of systems and to share best practices.

Ted Sapoznik, who is now president of the company's communication papers business, was at that time assigned to integrate Fort James's three paper plants in the West with the one Georgia-Pacific plant in the same region. He and a small team identified the main opportunities and then put together a synergy team to work on integration plans and action for each opportunity area—paper machines, converting, the staff functions, and so forth. Team members came from all four mills. As Sapoznik describes the effort, "I knew that the MIP process was the way to go even though I knew the timing would not be as short-term as the usual MIP process. But we did require specific goals, detailed work plans, regular progress reviews."

One of the synergy teams, for example, worked on fiber optimization. They agreed on overall manufacturing and wood procurement principles and on where to make and ship various fibers. They were able to drive overall region fiber costs to significantly lower levels than had been previously possible when the mills had been operating independently.

Sapoznik describes how the process contributed to broader issues: "From a strategic point of view, one team studied which machines we should run to maximize our returns. Again, they worked within the MIP discipline, but did not try to get their work done in a hundred days. It took much longer. But the result of that team's work was the decision to shut down the operation of one pulping line and four paper machines. Somebody joked that this analysis had been going on for fifteen years because the same issues had been on the table for that long, but had never been acted on. With the MIP discipline built in, we got it done in less than a year. And it had a major impact on our cost structure and bottom line."

Beyond the synergy teams, much of the gains in the acquisition came from the rapid introduction of the Mill Improvement Process in the Fort James mills. MIP specialists went to work with the new mills to help organize their wave improvement methodology. The ongoing rapid results process for improvement was the first commonly imposed cultural bridge linking the new facilities with the rest of Georgia-Pacific.

An Amazing Transformation: The Old Town Mill

The Mill Improvement Process played a critical role in the company's mill in Old Town, Maine. The mill, a comparatively small facility that had been operating for more than a hundred years, was facing some serious difficulties in 2002. In addition to the economic challenges of running an older plant in the northeast with high electric power costs, relationships with the union representing mill employees was at a low ebb. More than thirty unsettled grievances were waiting to be handled in arbitration. Negotiations with the union failed to produce a new contract so the workforce continued working with no contract. The union issued frequent flyers attacking the company and making clear their determination to block any efforts to improve productivity.

Facing costs that were too high and with no apparent way to reduce them, the company terminated the operations of the consumer products side of the mill (tissue, paper towels), laying off 300 workers. It continued the pulp mill, employing about 250.

Given the somewhat depressed state of the job market in northern Maine, the governor intervened. After several conferences involving the governor, union leadership, and mill management, the union leadership indicated a willingness to help the plant become more competitive. When the governor's request and the union's response were presented to Pete Correll, the company's CEO, he said that he was willing to give it a chance.

The consumer products side of the mill started up again almost immediately. Ralph Feck, then vice president of the Old Town Mill and now vice president of the company's Savannah River Mill operations, told the union leadership that the Mill Improvement Process would be the framework for the improvement effort. Still deeply suspicious of management, the union leaders agreed, but insisted that they themselves would be the employees who would participate. And so the diagnostic process was carried out by the plant managers and union leaders in the last quarter of 2002 and January 2003.

The diagnostics identified hundreds of potential productivity and quality improvements, and the steering committee—management and union leadership—selected eight to begin with.

While these initial projects were being carried out in various parts of the mill, a number of employees were drawn informally into the implementation process. And, with this experience, by the time the second round began, union leaders did not object to employees' being involved. Then the process began to accelerate. As one mill manager put it, "We had been used to looking at 2 percent, 3 percent, 4 percent improvements. In the first few months of the MIP, we achieved a 20 percent productivity improvement."

One early project, for example, aimed at reducing the time to change rolls on the paper-converting machines (machines that cut up the large paper rolls into the small finished product rolls). Typically the operator of a machine would make this change alone—even though it involved moving and installing a heavy roll, then threading the paper web through the machine. It took forty or forty-five minutes to do it. The team concluded that operators at nearby machines who might not be busy at the moment could come to help change the roll. This project not only significantly reduced the roll change time but also was the first of many job flexibility projects.

Teams experimented with ways to eliminate machine breakdowns. They experimented with new ways to maintain machinery. They experimented with ways to keep the machines and rollers clean to avoid contaminating the product. In all, during the first two years well over a hundred of these projects were carried out, plus an additional hundred or more "quick hits" that could be carried out and documented quickly without a formal team structure.

The result? An astounding 67 percent output increase, equal to millions of cases of products. And beyond the hard numbers, the culture of the mill was undergoing a radical transformation. As one manager describes it, "Grievances stopped. If you looked in at any of the project review sessions at the two-, six- and ten-week points, it was impossible to tell who were the production workers and who were the supervisors. They were all so wrapped up in the projects and their success."

When the program began, the superintendent in charge of the paper machines—the one professional papermaker in the mill—decided that he didn't want any part of employee participation in decisions. He walked out. It seemed unlikely that they would find a qualified papermaker who would give up another job to come to the northern Maine woods to work in a plant with a shaky future. "My heart stopped," says Ralph Feck. "The other managers too. Nobody could make paper like this guy." Management gathered the production workers together and asked for their ideas about what to do.

They asserted they could keep the mill going. So, with one of their members elected as a scheduling coordinator, the production workers ran the machines for seven months—all the while improving output and quality. A new papermaker was brought in at that time only because of the need to experiment with some major technical innovations that required specialized training.

The transformation from a mill that was in constant conflict to a mill in which employees shared significant responsibility with management took only a few months. Of all the cases cited in this book, it provides one of the most dramatic examples of how zest can release the hidden potential lurking just below the surface even when the environment is gloomiest.

Fifteen months after the union contract crisis, the process was continuing to move forward, launching wave after wave of projects. All the people in the mill, employees, supervisors, and union leaders alike, were working together with one goal in mind: to make the mill as competitive as possible. As mentioned, output rose about 67 percent in 2003. Halfway through 2004 the mill was on target to generate an additional 60 percent improvement—to a level almost triple the 2003 budget plan. Most of the employees have been actively engaged in the process.

The investment required to achieve these results? A modest amount of overtime pay when people occasionally had to come in for team meetings!

Feck, who has since been promoted to run a mill ten times the size of Old Town, sums it up this way: "It was just wonderful to see what people could do when we gave them the chance. It gave you goose bumps to walk through the mill and see them at it."

Ten Years of Progress

In 2004, when this is being written, the MIP has been operating on the production side of the business for a decade. During that time the process has contributed many hundreds of millions of dollars to the Georgia-Pacific bottom line. As to the continuing value-added of the process: when the benefits produced by additional capital investment are factored out of the calculations, the baseline year-over-year improvement for most of the company's facilities prior to introduction of MIP had been about 2.5 percent per year. In the eighteen to twenty-four months after introducing MIP to any mill this rate generally spiked to about 5.5 percent per year. It then settles back to a sustained level of about 3.5 percent—a rate 40 percent higher than the traditional rate of improvement. Compounding this differential in non–capital improvement against the competition is a powerful advantage and one that has allowed Georgia-Pacific to thrive in its highly competitive environment.

When applied at the facility level, the process fosters ownership and involvement of the entire workforce in driving improvement. It drives home the lesson that to improve a process, you need to involve and engage those doing the work. Georgia-Pacific has been careful to make sure that team initiatives do not result in a loss of jobs or employment. This is a tough challenge, but one that is vital to meet. The company feels that improvement is part of everybody's job and that improvement should lead not only to reduced costs and growth but also to greater job security.

All through the years, the improvement effort has been supported by a corporate staff group that has helped introduce MIP into new units, has supported collaboration across units, and has maintained consistency of the process. Charlie Hodges set a pattern of having this group divided, staffed partly by new recruits and partly by Georgia-Pacific people. These corporate specialists are indoctrinated by spending some time at headquarters reviewing various program materials and resources. Then they work on a large engagement as part of the support team. After two such engagements, each of which lasts about nine months, the specialist is ready to work independently.

Mill managers are expected to think strategically—in terms of the resources they control and what they can achieve by adding or subtracting resources. MIP focuses on making improvements by finding better methods that reduce usage, control waste, or improve production rates. With a close and continuing interaction between operational improvement on one hand and strategic planning on the other, as described in Chapter Ten, Georgia-Pacific provides an excellent example of a developmental approach to strategic progress.

Small Projects to Drive the Largest Changes

An illustration of how mill managers use the MIP to carve off achievable elements from even the most ambitious changes is occurring in 2004 at the Muskogee Mill in Oklahoma. Even though much of their energy is focused on the short-range MIP process, mill VP Karl Meyers and the mill's management team meet every week for two hours in a session dedicated to a further-out look— "Where do we want to be in six months, and beyond?"

One outcome of these sessions was the decision to reengineer the entire manufacturing process to ensure the maximum exploitation of the very costly equipment—with 100 percent operation seven days a week, twenty-four hours a day, as the ideal goal. Instead of doing it as a typical big-fix reengineering project, it is being tackled as a series of rapid results projects. There are a hundred production lines in the converting mill, and one team will tackle each line. Thirty or forty of these teams will be launched in each wave. Eventually about 180 teams will have taken part in the mapping and redesigning of all the process flows in the converting mill and related operations. As Karl Meyers describes the progress, "By the end of July 2004, three pilot line teams had been through the process. The total uptime of those lines had increased—in six weeks—from 49 percent to 62 percent. So it is a 25 percent increase in a few weeks' time. If similar results are achieved in subsequent waves, the potential is for many millions of dollars of benefit."

New Applications to Other Business Dimensions

Early in 2000 the company began taking the rapid-cycle mode of attack into other functions of the business. There are two components here. One parallels the mill improvement process; people who do the work in Sales, Customer Service, Marketing, and other functions are now improving their work processes. The other component is the way they are applying this process to strategic issues and are launching teams of managers working on better use of resources. Teams in this category have eliminated unneeded machinery and have found ways to achieve needed output with smaller staffs. These teams have been highly successful—without destroying the "no job loss" relationship.

Ted Sapoznik, president of the Communication Papers business, puts it this way: "On Strategy: We are trying to turn the paper business around to become much more profitable. We've identified four 'strategic planks' and within each plank we are using MIP project teams to drive progress. We have a 'core team' or steering committee running each plank, and each steering committee appoints a team to work on each of the areas in its plank that requires an action plan. So here again, we have adopted the disciplines of the MIP to execute a business strategy."

In the fall of 2003, Georgia-Pacific started doing business-level diagnostic work to get at businesswide revenue and cost opportunities as well as opportunities for greater synergy. Wave teams at corporate headquarters were launched and followed the standard kickoff process followed by two-, six-, and ten-week review formats. Within the first two waves, this Business Improvement Process (BIP) yielded more than $100 million in documented, sustainable benefit. The first wave launched fifteen teams in the retail tissue business; the second had fifty-four teams engaging 550 individuals from the retail, commercial, and Dixie businesses combined.

The process is continuing to expand, driving strategy through study teams and quickly capturing value through breakthrough teams. Each quarter, the individual business steering teams determine wave teams and team membership. They launch teams and oversee the two-week review. Six-week reviews of team results are attended by the presidents of each business. The final ten-week review is attended by the company's two top officers, Pete Correll and President Lee Thomas. Participation is so extensive and the scope of improvements so great that the reviews span two to three days and are webcast over the corporation's intranet so that mill managers can participate.

The business-level diagnostics now focus on four categories: customers, products, assets, and productivity. As the implementation phase began, these same categories became "pillars" for the improvement strategy. Each customer team, for example, focuses on how to reduce costs or find other ways to improve value for a single customer. The products teams focus on the profitability of specific product families or items and how to engineer improvements that increase value to the customer or reduce costs to Georgia-Pacific, or both. Asset teams focus on how to best allocate production assets, shifting manufacture to those most productive and eliminating high-cost assets from service. Finally, productivity teams focus on identifying the current lowest-cost production assets in the company and work on improving them even further.

Improvement Is Totally Routine

For many organizations, change is undertaken at certain moments when the need is urgent. But, as emphasized earlier, no matter how good a change concept may be, if the organization lacks implementation capability, the effort is apt to turn into a futile crisis. It is the lack of a continuing improvement effort that drives so many organizations to engage consultants for the ambitious, big-fix solutions that are intended to solve everything—but rarely solve much of anything.

For Georgia-Pacific, change and improvement is now part of the daily routine. Day by day, implementation capability has been building across the corporation in every function at every level. Visibility of the process is kept very high, at both the facility and the corporate levels. The process, by its nature, focuses on results. No one believes that the mere description of an opportunity means anything unless it is keyed to what the team is going to do about it.

For many years the company quietly concentrated on learning to apply the methodology successfully and did not publicize its success. But by 2002, Pete Correll and Lee Thomas began talking about the process to the investment community. By 2003, the process was being described in company advertising.

While the fundamental structure of the improvement efforts has been relatively stable, it has not been static. Diagnostic approaches have changed and evolved. Occasionally, a facility needs to step back once again, as in the original diagnostic, to fully analyze the situation and generate a new pool of ideas. Over the years, the corporate MIP specialist support group has always supported the initiation of the process in the business units. One or several specialists work in the operation from the initial diagnostic through the second wave. The size of the group expands or shrinks, reflecting the demand for new engagements or diagnostic support. As the corporate level started on the Business Improvement Process, an intranet Web site was developed with the various templates and a file system to support the common methodology and consistent reporting structure. That tool has helped to drive more rapid and better compliance with structure for new users, and is being further developed to help provide a common hub for all teams. The corporate MIP specialist group now focuses primarily on collaboration and diagnostic support.

Charlie Hodges, the first leader of the corporate MIP specialist group and now vice president of the company's Crossett, Arkansas, operations, sums up one of the most profound effects of the process: "Our whole mentality about capital has changed. For example, once we would have felt that a 55 percent utilization rate on converting lines was OK. Now we expect 70 percent. When improvement is needed, instead of thinking of new investment, we think about getting better results from the investment we have. This is true all across the corporation." And Rick Larrick, who has been managing the corporate MIP staff, adds, "Rapid-cycle improvement is a simple concept. The greatest danger to its successful implementation is that new people in leadership roles want to make it more complicated. Georgia-Pacific has done a grand job of keeping the methodology simple and pure to the essential results—achieving rapid-cycle projects."

Key Points

- The Georgia-Pacific process began in two mills, following a thorough diagnosis of opportunities.

- CEO Correll expressed impatience with mere diagnosis— he demanded some action. Rapid results projects were launched with considerable success.

- The process was formalized into a ten-week process with diagnosis, rapid results projects, and sustainability planning.

- As the process migrated across the company employee involvement was increasingly widespread, with more cross-functional and multilevel teams.

- A collaborative network was established with increasing amounts of sharing of information among mills.

- Senior management attention and widespread sharing of performance information encourages constant striving and innovation.

Part Three

USING ENHANCED IMPLEMENTATION CAPABILITY TO EXECUTE LARGE-SCALE CHANGE

Part Three describes how to exploit the momentum of rapid successes and the increasing mastery over the change process in achieving the really big changes. It illustrates the application of the process to mergers and acquisitions, to strategic change, and to the execution of difficult change in developing countries. Then it details how rapid results projects can serve as the core of a results-focused approach to the development of leadership competence.

8

MAKE ACQUISITIONS AND MERGERS SUCCEED

Few changes that managers have to carry out are as complex and challenging as mergers and acquisitions. Large numbers of people in two different organizations are suddenly plunged into an entirely new working environment in which many of the policies, programs, work routines, personal relationships, and habits—the supports that provide regularity and guidance in people's daily work—are abruptly dissolved. A whole new set of work processes and relationships must be created and made operative almost at once. It is an enormous challenge and one that many fail to overcome. Because of the daunting scope and pace of the changes that must be carried out simultaneously, managers often feel that master planning and large-scale policy making are the keys to success. But unless master planning is linked to and supported by many small-scale, rapid-cycle projects, the weaknesses inherent in large-scale changes can easily undermine success.

A Dismal Track Record

Despite the hopes and aspirations that characterize every new merger and acquisition, most such deals are, statistically speaking, doomed from the start. *BusinessWeek* in 2002 reported that 61 percent of acquirers destroyed their own shareholders' value. In a 2003 *Harvard Business Review* article, Larry Selden, a Columbia

SUZANNE C. FRANCIS, lead author; Katherine Paul-Chowdhury and Matthew K. McCreight provided case material.

University finance professor emeritus, and Geoffrey Colvin, a senior editor-at-large at *Fortune* magazine, estimated the failure rate at 70 percent to 80 percent.[1]

Acquisitions and mergers are like marriages. People have fantasies about life after the knot is tied, but in neither the corporate nor the personal world is a change in legal status any guarantee of living happily ever after. Too few business executives who are engaged in romancing the object of their acquisitive desires do what needs to be done to ensure successful merging. The business news is full of stories blaming M&A problems on the follies of senior executives overly fascinated with doing deals. Some suggest that acquisitions might be more successful if the deals were financed differently or if the rationale for mergers was strategically more sound. But the evidence suggests that poor strategic fit and overpayment for acquired assets are less frequently the cause of failures compared to the lack of properly managing what happens after the deal is done.

In today's business world, acquisitions and mergers are the best illustrations of how often the big bets can create high expectations of success that fail to materialize. The excitement of the chase is followed by the sobering challenge of making the combined business run effectively. Sadly, it turns out that business marriages have about the same success rate as human ones in the United States.

Why So Little Success?

The common characteristics of mergers and acquisitions—and major organizational restructuring as well—are the size, the shock impact, and the scope of the changes required. In most cases, the big decisions are made by a few people at the highest reaches of the organization. To those people, when the deal is closed it marks the end of a job well done. They declare victory and start to move on.

But making the merged organization actually work is the job of other people. To those other people the announcement of a merger is not the end of the drama but merely the end of act one. Act two, where they will have to play the starring roles, covers the integration of the acquisition—and the challenge can be far greater than that of negotiating the deal.

A successful integration process requires hundreds or thousands of micro-connections to be severed and then rewired. These changes take place in the structure, social systems, information flows, and work procedures. Because of their sheer numbers and the dynamic and changing environment where they take place, they cannot be planned and mandated in advance. Instead, success requires hundreds or thousands of initiatives by people who have the skill, the context, the authority, and the capability to make decisions on their own.

It should come as no surprise that one of the major reasons for the poor track record for M&A deals is the lack of a sound methodology for carrying out all those essential changes. Moreover, even where a decent plan exists on paper, the organization's implementation capability may not be adequate to make the plan succeed. Sometimes the managers in charge simply assume that, as people get used to being in the new situation, everyone will eventually figure out what to do. For example, one serial acquirer purchased three similar software businesses. Instead of trying to mesh them or reshape them, they were all left to keep up the good performance they had been showing. But after a few years, overall financial performance was well below targets; customers were complaining repeatedly about long installation times and inadequate support services, and one business had too many people while another was struggling to get the work done with too few.

Sometimes companies go through the motions without sufficient commitment to make it happen. For example, top managers of one high-tech business named a senior staff person to lead a new integration. He arrived at the acquired company the next day, but no one there knew who he was or why he was there. From there, things went downhill. He worked valiantly to create a plan for retaining the technical staff who were needed to develop some new products (the primary reason for the acquisition). At the end of three months the integration process was declared complete, and he was moved to a new assignment. Despite his best efforts, the product introduction was way off schedule, and more than a third of the critical technical talent had fled to other companies.

Sad as these failure stories may be, they might have become successes had the senior management team done some thinking, early in the negotiations, about the nature of the changes that would be required once the deal was complete and what it would actually take to make those changes happen.

Fulfilling the Promise

The first element of an effective integration process is a clear definition of what overall aims the merger or acquisition is intended to fulfill. Call it a vision or an overall objective, it defines how the marriage is intended to advance the life of the enterprise. The second element is a set of specific action plans—a description of what must be done, when, and by whom. And third is the launching of a series of rapid-cycle projects aimed at achieving tangible benefits as rapidly as possible. In addition to generating rapid results, these disciplined short-term projects provide on-the-ground testing of what it will take to ensure overall success. From our experience with hundreds of deals in dozens of companies, these are the three key interrelated steps, as illustrated in Figure 8.1, that must play out together—with rapid results as a critical component.

From the moment each project is launched, the results will not be exactly as planned. As experience develops, the action plans must be modified to reflect the realities of the changing situation. And thus it goes—actual field experience provides the reality data to modify the plans; the modified plans provide the new directions for action. It is a continuous action-learning process, and the greater the skill of the organization in modifying plans to reflect reality the greater its chances of success.

In the case of an acquisition or merger, this continuous action-learning capability needs to be created at breakneck speed—in weeks and months rather than years. Once a deal is announced,

Figure 8.1   Three Elements of Integration

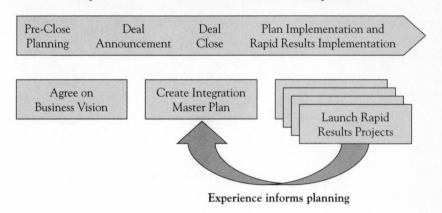

Experience informs planning

economic value (including stock price) dissipates with every day that the synergistic assumptions of the deal are not actually realized. So change capability, on a very wide scale, becomes critical.

Here is how these three elements work out in practice:

Creating the Overall Vision

What's needed is a clear picture of what the company is trying to do—and what the integrated organization should look like at the end of twelve or eighteen months.

A growth or market strategy that calls for expansion through acquisition frequently gives rise to not one but a series of acquisitions over a period of years. Decisions about which parts of the business will have the greatest gains from an acquisition and which opportunities to go after must be linked to the strategic intent.

In other words, strategy formulation points the way to specific acquisitions. Once the strategy has been set, decisions about where acquisitions fit and which ones should be pursued can lead to the creation of deals intended to help the company accomplish one or more strategic goals. A loose consensus on the kinds of acquisitions needed is not enough; the key to success is a written statement hammered out among the senior leaders of what the combined business must look like in twelve to eighteen months. Creating that vision is a crucial step in setting the stage for success.

Since acquisitions and mergers are often opportunistic, no purchase can ever match the desired specifications exactly. And that means that this vision creation must be carefully honed—even on a unit-by-unit basis—to match the reality of the purchase rather than the wish list that led to the offer.

That initial vision sets the rough direction and pace for changes that must take place in business strategy, operations, organization structure, and financial performance to realize the potential expected from the deal.

Creating the Master Integration Plan

In the planning stage of an acquisition integration or transformation, it is critical that the appropriate cross-functional team develop a set of detailed plans that lay out the steps that will be taken in order to create the combined business envisioned for the deal. Such a plan needs to include explicit targets for results to be generated. These plans provide a road map for the implementation work, and they include key action steps and who will drive each of them. They also create the agenda for a variety of policy dialogues. Senior leadership, for example, needs to identify the key top-level decisions and when each of those decisions must be made.

As we have pointed out elsewhere, it is unrealistic to expect the managers who will be *running* the integrated business to be responsible for implementing the integration at the same time.[2] Even while the vision is being created, and certainly by the time the master plan is being designed, an integration manager needs to be appointed. This manager will see to it that all the integration efforts are organized and will carry out a number of the integration tasks—such as launching rapid results projects and helping to design the master plan.

Further elements of that plan include the spelling out of resource requirements. Thoughtful dialogue is needed across various business areas to resolve sequencing issues, personnel assignments, and potential resource bottlenecks. In addition, the plan needs to spell out the nature of the communication with key constituencies, both internal and external, that will best support the effort.

The creation of the implementation plan makes it possible to form integration teams with specific assignments to tackle major action elements. Acquisitions invite scrutiny from the investment community and force a business to commit to accomplishing specific results. This is actually a healthy influence since so many acquisition integration goals are defined in purely activities-oriented generalities. It is critical that the master integration plan clearly specify the measurable results that will be attained in the first month of the integration and every month thereafter.

Milestones for the most important steps in the plan must be included. These steps include any reorganization such as consolidating sales forces or integrating additional products into an existing manufacturing facility. With the initial vision and the detailed integration plan as guides, the risk of confusion when the announcement is made is significantly reduced.

Launching Immediate Action—Rapid Results Projects to Fuel the Fire

Results-focused rapid-cycle projects provide the necessary action complement to the master integration plans. They are an effective mechanism for getting done what needs to be done and for achieving the necessary bottom-line results from the very first day. These projects also provide the opportunity for testing new ways of working together and structuring work processes before rolling them out to the entire merged organizations. Finally, these projects serve as a flexible, real-time mechanism for discovering what is going to be required to make the change succeed. The experiences of the early weeks will naturally reveal all sorts of unanticipated challenges. Instead of being thrown off-course by these surprises, management can use the learning that comes from early experiences and channel it back into a revised master plan.

Consider the case of JLG Industries, a $1.3 billion company that manu-factures aerial work platforms and telescoping materials handlers. JLG acquired the Omniquip family of products from Textron, a competitor, but did not acquire the Omniquip production facilities. Thus after the acquisition it had to move five manufacturing lines from two different facilities to its own manufacturing site—and do so within six months. The integration team did a significant amount of overall planning for what needed to be done in terms of time frames, production locations, production volumes, and quality standards. To minimize the risk of large-scale errors, the team decided to treat these moves as a series of mini-projects rather than as a single massive project with thou-sands of steps that all had to be monitored simultaneously.

As the first mini-project they laid out a detailed plan to move the first production line. As soon as that line was in place, they started it up and built "machine #1." That was less than sixty days after the launch of the integration team. The aim was to learn what further refinements were needed. As they went through the intensive process of moving the first production line and producing the first machine, they learned things they never could have anticipated. This included new insights into requirements for parts numbering, into how to main-tain an adequate supply of spare parts, and into the differences between engineering drawings and the reality of how the acquired machines were actually built.

With that first line serving as their rapid-cycle success, they modi-fied their master plans and began to implement the moves for the other four lines as a series of discrete subprojects. The entire task was accomplished in less time than had been budgeted, and every-thing was in place and working smoothly on schedule.

As the JLG case illustrates, not only is effective implementa-tion necessary, *rapid-cycle* implementation is critically important. It reduces the risk of significant errors or breakdowns by making sure all systems are tested in microcosm before full implementation. And the rapid results projects provide fast feedback on the effectiveness of changes being made. Finally, rapid results projects increase the energy, creativity, and motivation that people bring to the effort and reduce the toll on employees' productivity, health, and personal lives.

Rapid results are critical for another reason. Because many acquisitions fail to deliver the expected performance, an acquiring company's stock price typically declines after it announces an acquisition. In addition, companies may have assumed a lot of debt to finance a major acquisition, and this increases investor anxiety. Tangible results early in the game—and in line with the rosy promises—do much to minimize the effects of this pessimism. Another benefit from achieving the acquisition's benefits earlier is that the total dollar value over time will be higher.

Developing Acquisition Integration Capability

This constant interplay between the master integration plans and the rapid results implementation projects provides continuous learning for the participating managers—and it tests methodologies that can be used over and over again in successive integrations.

For a number of companies, this learning process begins with a series of smaller acquisitions. Later, when a huge, hard-to-digest acquisition comes along, the company has the tools, methods, and internal capability to successfully tackle a far more difficult challenge. This "serial acquisition" approach allows companies to practice and learn from smaller, lower-risk deals, while creating the capability that will allow them to do much bigger deals eventually.

The experience of MeadWestvaco illustrates this process clearly.

MeadWestvaco: A Cycle of Success

On August 29, 2001, one of the news items in the *New York Times* was the announcement that the Mead Corporation and Westvaco Corporation—with combined revenues of $8 billion—had agreed to a merger.[3] This deal had been a well-kept secret within both companies so, except for a handful of people on each side, it was a complete surprise when these two large paper and packaging companies announced they were tying the knot. Only the most creative thinkers among employees and investors would have imagined a merger of these two competitors. Yet once the news became public, nearly everyone agreed that it was a good strategic move.

Included in the merger announcement was the appointment of Jim Buzzard, then the number two executive in Westvaco, as the leader of the integration effort. It was his job to manage the integration and produce $325 million of incremental profit improvement—resulting from synergies between the companies—within twenty-four months, as promised in the merger announcement. This was a daunting goal, made all the more challenging because the deal was being executed as a "merger of equals," the toughest model of all for successful integration.

The merger was officially closed on January 30, 2002. Within fifteen months the actual profit improvements were on track to exceed the targeted $325 million by more than $75 million. Moreover, the merger had been so well implemented that when Jim Buzzard moved out of the integration job to become president of the combined company he was not replaced, and the integration office was closed.

What was it that enabled this most challenging merger to succeed with apparent ease where so many fail?

One of the most important ingredients was the development of integration competence before this enormous merger was attempted, and the continued development of integration competence while the merger was being carried out.

Early Learning: The Evadale Acquisition

In the late 1990s, Westvaco acquired a $100 million pharmaceutical packaging company. Some planning was done after the acquisition was announced, but it was not a very thorough job. Moreover, most of the planning was done by Westvaco people with the expectation that the acquired organization would follow the plans when instructed.

At about the same time, Westvaco announced its intent to purchase a paperboard mill in Evadale, Texas. Eager to benefit from the earlier experience, John Luke, Westvaco's CEO at the time, assigned Ronnie Hise, a research manager in the Packaging Resources Group, to take charge of planning for this one. Hise gathered a small Westvaco team, along with the Evadale mill manager and a few of his associates who knew the deal was being negotiated—a group of around ten people who performed what they called an "expanded due diligence." They identified about twenty-five major opportunities to reduce costs and increase productivity. This team, unlike the one in the earlier acquisition, was cross-functional and included a number of people from the acquired organization.

As soon as the acquisition was announced, a larger team was assembled to develop action plans for implementing the profit-enhancing opportunities identified by the small planning team. For example, Evadale had traditionally taken two weeks of shutdown each year for maintenance and overhaul of its machinery. One of the first rapid results projects aimed to reduce the time required for that maintenance shutdown. The team reviewed best practices collected both from Evadale and other Westvaco mills and took some immediate steps to incorporate several of the shutdown tasks into regular routines that ran every week or every two weeks. Some other steps aimed at improving the efficiency of the procedures used during the summer shutdown. Less than six months after the acquisition, annual maintenance was being done in one week of downtime rather than two. The result of this and several other successful rapid results projects was that the projected profit enhancements from the acquisition were quickly exceeded.

Two months after the deal's closing, managers from both companies who had been active in the integration met for two days to assess progress and plan next steps. Instead of congratulating themselves on how good a job they had done, they analyzed how the integration had gone and what they might have done better.

Ronnie Hise, who was moving into a new job, carried out one final act as integration manager: he gathered the findings of this two-day conference and codified it as part of the integration database for the company. He included an archive that documented the work done at Evadale. This included the plans for "expanded due diligence," the integration report to the executive team, and samples of communications that had been effective. He also compiled—for use by future integration managers—various analytic and planning templates and tools that had been used as part of the database. Thus Westvaco began developing its integration capability as a core competence.

Practice Makes More Perfect: The IMPAC Acquisition

Then, in 2000, Westvaco acquired a $350 million high-end packaging company, IMPAC. This acquisition was much more complex than its predecessors: IMPAC was an international company with design, marketing, sales, and manufacturing in a number of countries. Moreover, both the pharmaceutical packaging company previously acquired and Westvaco's Consumer Packaging Division were to be combined with IMPAC. Joe Wong, one of the leaders of research for the Specialty Chemicals Division, took on the integration leadership with a small staff and formed several cross-functional and international working teams.

One of those joint teams, focused on purchasing activities, set a goal of reducing total purchasing expenditures by 5 percent. The team analyzed and renegotiated contracts to consolidate their inks and coatings purchases from two suppliers. This one step yielded a $285,000 annual benefit within a hundred days.

One of the key values of detailed integration master planning surfaced in this integration. Everything seemed to be going well, but after about five months, it became clear that the actual sales results would fall short of forecast sales. John Luke told the integration team that he would not revise the goal: the forecast sales results must be achieved. He assigned them the task of planning how to do it and then reporting their plans to him. In response, one cross-unit sales team identified specific opportunities among the top thirty consumer packaging customers where they believed that a unified approach by several of the businesses working jointly could win additional sales. Experimenting with new joint approaches to their sales strategies and with some unique packaging solutions, they quantified a plan to achieve 10 percent growth with their top thirty customers. Within several months, they exceeded that target by applying these strategies with their top five consumer packaging customers.

During the entire IMPAC integration, Joe Wong assessed how the integration was progressing and what they were learning. He added these insights to the internal Web site he had been developing to provide tools and templates to a widely dispersed integration team. It was also used to collect integration plans and updates for regularly scheduled teleconference reviews. The company was treating acquisition integration as a core competence it wanted to develop.

Success Is No Accident:
The MeadWestvaco Experience

The learning from these smaller acquisitions proved invaluable when Westvaco Corporation merged with Mead.

Shortly after the announcement, the senior management team, comprising six senior executives from each company, came together for a special work session. Their job was to create the vision—what MeadWestvaco was to look like in a year—and to begin sketching out the assignments for the major areas of the master integration plan. Jim Buzzard, as mentioned earlier, was made integration leader with a small staff from both companies—including Ronnie Hise. Members of this staff were to be the integration consultants, each working with a number of different functions and business groups. Insights from the databases and Web sites created during earlier acquisitions were incorporated into an integration planning workbook.

Each consultant worked with a set of internal clients to shape the detailed master integration plans for their business unit or corporate staff function and to complete immediate action plans. Most of this work was designed as a series of rapid-cycle, results-focused implementation projects, with thirty-, sixty-, and ninety-day progress checkpoints.

For example, both companies were in the midst of an ERP installation. The joint team on IT consolidation quickly reached consensus on how to proceed. The combined company had more data centers than it needed, so one of the team's initial projects was to determine the best locations for data centers to support the ERP strategy. Within four months of the closing, the team had completed the first consolidation of two data centers into one.

The managers planning the integration knew that purchasing would have many synergies after the merger, but before the deal was officially consummated, they were separate companies and could not legally discuss pricing and other relevant issues. The creative solution: a "clean room" was established, and a small number of retired purchasing professionals from both companies were hired and assigned the job of doing all the research needed to exploit purchasing synergies once the deal was closed. One firm ground rule was that there could be absolutely no communication between this study team and the acquisition team. The other ground rule was that implementation had to start immediately after the close. Thus, by the time the deal closed, the team had reviewed vendor relationships and an action plan was in place. All this added up to accelerated results—with savings accrued much faster than expected.

Three months after closing, a cross-business development team with sales and marketing representation from all divisions was charged with accelerating top-line revenue growth. A target of $25 million incremental sales was established for the last eight months of the year. One of the first rapid results projects had two divisions, Packaging Systems and Coated Board, collaborating on a proposal to jointly supply certain requirements of Unilever. Previously only Packaging Systems had been supplying those products, but the benefits of expanding the relationship with an existing supplier quickly became clear to Unilever. And that enabled the two divisions to beat out a competitor and win the contract for nearly $4 million in incremental business over the next eighteen months. The team achieved its initial rapid results goals and continues today, more than three years after the deal closed, working on more complex multidivision product development and sales efforts.

Looking back on the experience as head of the office of integration, Jim Buzzard summarizes his perspective on the experience:

> The first thing that contributed to our success was selecting experienced, respected operating people as full-time staff for the Office of Integration and for integration team leaders. That gave us credibility with the rest of the organization even when our decisions were personally painful.
>
> Coming to agreement on standard processes was key to moving ahead quickly. In a matter of a few weeks, the Office of Integration laid out the planning templates and deliverables each team would be asked to produce for the ten-, thirty-, and sixty-day plan reviews. While it may sound rigid, it kept the thinking organized and the work focused on the deadlines without inhibiting creativity. In about twelve weeks, between mid-October and early January, we completed the overall plan and had executive team approval to start implementation immediately after the deal closed at the end of January. It was a stretch to meet that deadline, but we were ready to go.
>
> The synergy targets were set and then negotiated into specific goals for each team. Since the same team was responsible for both the planning and the implementation, they had accountability for a plan that would produce results on the timetable they set. We quickly learned not to overplan. Get it 80 percent right and then drive for results. To hit the synergy goals on schedule, final changes were made as the plans were carried out.

The success of this merger vividly illustrates the power of using small-step successes to learn how to take the larger steps—and then breaking the larger steps again into hundred-day projects. Imagine if MeadWestvaco had tried to carry out this merger with the competence level it had when it purchased the small pharmaceutical packaging company just a few years previously.

ArvinMeritor: Putting the Parts Together

Meritor Automotive took a pathway similar to Westvaco's. Having been spun off from Rockwell Automotive as an independent supplier of components for the automobile industry, Meritor had little experience with acquisitions. In fact, one of the senior executives joked that when the company was with Rockwell, it had been in "acquisition jail." Thus it had neither a process nor the widespread capability needed to integrate new companies, even though merging was a key requirement for success in an industry with overcapacity and the need for consolidation.

To develop this capacity, Larry Yost, CEO at the time, embarked on a series of small acquisitions over a period of two years. First Meritor bought Volvo's heavy-duty valve business in Sweden, essentially a single plant. Then the company bought the brake parts business from Lucas Varity—a somewhat larger acquisition that involved multiple locations in Europe and the United States. Another acquisition was Euclid Auto Parts, a replacement parts supplier based in Cleveland, Ohio.

For each of these acquisitions, Yost commissioned his head of business development, Juan De La Riva, to not just integrate the acquisitions but develop a replicable process that would create the capability to do future acquisitions more easily. At the heart of this process were multiple teams that had to accomplish waves of hundred-day rapid results projects for the integrations. For example, one of the teams in the Swedish acquisition figured out how to use a special heat-treating technology in the new plant to produce components for other Meritor operations in Europe. This move generated substantial operational savings. A team in the Lucas Varity acquisition accelerated the consolidation of financial reporting, allowing Meritor to shut down an acquired site earlier than planned.

Over the course of two years, hundreds of old and new Meritor people gained experience in setting goals, creating plans, and dealing with all the change issues associated with generating rapid results.

All this learning and capability development proved to be essential when, in late 2000, Meritor agreed to a "merger of equals" with another automotive parts company, Arvin Industries, creating a $7.5 billion company called ArvinMeritor. Instead of starting from scratch, Meritor had a replicable process and confidence that hundreds of people could actively tackle the integration challenges. Thus Larry Yost, who became the CEO of the new company, was able to quickly bring together his new senior team to shape a vision of the combined companies.

In the space of two weeks, he launched twenty integration teams focusing on both synergy and growth targets. Each team, most of which included people who had been involved in one of the earlier acquisitions, quickly carved out hundred-day goals and got moving. Juan De La Riva, who had supported the process for several previous acquisitions, organized the integration process. And the senior team, including new members from Arvin, had a tried-and-true way of reviewing progress weekly, reallocating resources, and making fast decisions. The result was that the integration process proceeded far faster than had originally been planned; synergy targets were met or exceeded, and the new company got off to a faster start than would have happened otherwise.

Lessons for Large-Scale Changes Within a Company

Organizations often carry out large-scale reorganizations and other changes that rival mergers and acquisitions in complexity and impact. The principles outlined in this chapter apply equally well in these situations. Here's an example:

At the start of 2000, Johnson & Johnson began integrating its two major pharmaceutical R&D groups. One of the first groups selected to form a single global organization with common processes, standards, and skills was the Quality Assurance function of Clinical R&D, led by Tom Kirsch.

Quality Assurance carries out some very challenging tasks in association with Clinical R&D. They must respond to tight deadlines and always be prepared for unannounced inspections by regulatory agencies. Their work can influence the fate of multibillion-dollar products.

The two organizations coming together had two major locations in Europe and three in the United States responsible for the quality assurance of dozens of clinical trials of promising new drugs around the world. Not only did the two groups differ but the individual locations within each group had their own unique work processes and systems.

To minimize the time and energy that the integration would require, QA leader Tom Kirsch and his management team decided to run it as they would an external merger—with an emphasis on rapid-cycle projects. They decided to focus first on how QA did their audits of clinical trials and on two other business processes. They started in just one of Kirsch's four functional groups. For each process they assigned a team with the following goals:

- To develop a new common and improved global process (including the necessary tools and materials)
- To gain management team approval for all the standard operating procedures, tools, and materials
- To train all staff and have the new processes in use

And do all that within a hundred days.

At the time, this objective seemed almost unattainable. The teams were launched in a work session in Belgium. In three days, they mapped the current processes and developed a set of new global processes as well as the plans for shifting to these processes. During the hundred days, team members worked with each other via e-mail, conference calls, and videoconferences. At the midway point the teams reassembled to assess progress and to plan the final push.

When the team that was focused on developing a standard best-practice process for auditing clinical trials developed a new process and communicated it, all the groups served by QA finally understood more exactly what the QA people did in their audits. In addition to achieving this clarity, the time for audits was reduced by more than 30 percent—a huge gain in productivity. The other teams also achieved their "impossible" goals, and the new processes were being put to immediate use.

Shortly thereafter, a second wave of process teams was launched in a similar fashion, and after them a third. And then the other major functional groups all launched their own rapid-cycle integration efforts—combining all their processes in two hundred-day cycles.

Since that time, Clinical R&D QA has become a source of ongoing innovation. In the following two years, they have integrated the Clinical QA functions of three major J&J acquisitions around the globe, all with increasing ease and effectiveness.

Conclusion

Companies can treat mergers, acquisitions, and major transformations somewhat as improvisational theater—doing the best they can, modifying the process day by day as they gain experience and explaining why it can't possibly be done better. Or they can recognize that they need some skill and methodology—and work to develop both. One critical key to success here is to use rapid results projects as the learning vehicle.

Chapter Nine shows how these same principles apply to generating effective action in some other very large-scale social and organizational change: issues of public health and economic development in countries of the developing world.

Key Points

- Mergers and acquisitions are among the most popular of the big-fix strategies.

- Despite the high hopes that accompany each of them, many actually destroy shareholder value—because companies do not have the implementation capacity to make them succeed.

- To change the odds, three elements are needed:

  A vision of what the organization should look like
  in twelve to eighteen months after the merger
  A detailed plan for how that can be achieved
  A series of rapid results projects

- These rapid results project produce rapid payback; they develop implementation capacity, and they provide vital experience for modifying the action plans.

- It's good to start with a few smaller acquisitions to develop acquisition integration capacity before going for the big one.

- The same approach can be applied to internal reorganizations, which are often similar to mergers or acquisitions.

9

UNLEASH IMPLEMENTATION CAPACITY IN DEVELOPING COUNTRIES

Over the past sixty years, developed countries have poured hundreds of billions of dollars into helping the developing countries of the world escape the trap of poverty, disease, and lack of hope. This aid has come through direct grants and through organizations such as the World Bank, the United Nations Development Program, regional development banks, and a variety of nongovernmental organizations. Unfortunately, while a small number of countries such as South Korea and China have emerged with viable economies, far more have sunk deeper into debt and have seen larger portions of their populations fall into poverty. Despite a level of investment unprecedented in human history, success stories are few and far between.

Of the many inexorable forces contributing to this failure, one key factor is the weakness in implementation capacity in the developing countries. The same assumptions that drive the push for big-fix solutions in business also underlie most economic and social development programs. Economists, agronomists, social scientists, and other experts develop large-scale recommendations for change and present them to the governments of client countries. The programs usually involve large projects, changes in regulations and laws, introduction of new technology, large-scale training and education, and government restructuring. Meanwhile, each country's leaders embark on similar large-scale programs, and commit their own precious resources—both human and capital—to pursue them.

Nadim F. Matta, lead author.

Sound and informed as these programs might be, their success requires tremendous implementation capacity at both the governmental and local levels—capacity that has rarely been developed and honed sufficiently to bring about the desired changes. This "capacity gap" sabotages social and economic progress in developing countries much as it does in individual business organizations.

In recent years, development professionals have begun to focus on implementation capacity as a key lever for effective social and economic transformation. In this chapter, we describe how government officials in developing countries, supported by the World Bank and other international and local development agencies, are beginning to use rapid results as a vehicle for unleashing implementation capacity in their countries.

The experiences we describe do not yet pass the test of institutionalized, irreversible change, but they offer a glimpse into the possibilities for making a sustained impact. The emerging rapid results stories from Nicaragua, Eritrea, Kenya, and other counties shed light on a possible path toward higher returns on investments in international development work.

The challenges tackled in these countries are diverse: fighting HIV/AIDS, increasing agricultural productivity, and accelerating economic growth. What all the experiences have in common is that their strategy is being guided by the pursuit of locally defined, hundred-day results-producing projects—called in these developing country pursuits *Rapid-Results Initiatives*. In this chapter, we describe how the proper context for these initiatives can be established and illustrate how they play a critical role in creating a virtuous cycle of results achievement and capacity enhancement.

The Bottom Line in Nicaragua— Pigs Are Getting Fatter

A large-scale project aimed at increasing the productivity of 120,000 farmers in the country by 30 percent within sixteen years had been launched in Nicaragua. The project seemed to have all the right elements built into it: strengthening quasi-government institutions, directing research on farmer productivity, stimulating a private sector market for provision of technical advice to farmers, building an information system to link R&D efforts with farmer needs, and others. Moreover, each of these elements (or project components) was being pursued by a diligent and committed team.

Yet two years into the effort, there was little visible impact on farmers. The project activities were mostly preparatory—geared to getting the systems, processes, and institutions in place. This omission is what caught the attention of the minister of agriculture. It was also on the mind of Norman Piccioni, the World Bank team leader in charge of the project. He had the uneasy feeling that apart from himself and the newly appointed minister, no one working on the project was losing sleep over the fact that no farmers had yet been touched by the effort.

Piccioni decided that he could not afford to wait. He knew that all the activities that had been mapped out in the sixteen-year project were necessary for achieving the hoped-for outcomes, but without some near-term impact he felt that the long-term project was at risk. There were already some indications that the minister might pull the plug on it. And Piccioni was increasingly concerned that without some change, all the activities and the good intentions behind them might not get translated into actual results.

Piccioni assembled all the stakeholders involved in the effort and shared with them the idea of mobilizing cross-functional teams and challenging them to achieve real results that would have an actual impact on farmers in the following hundred days.

The first workshop in the country, attended by thirty representatives from the various institutions—the "extended leadership group"—got off to a rocky start. The first agenda item was a discussion of the implementation risks and challenges, and the participants grabbed the opportunity to put on the table their frustrations about each other and about the development agencies that were funding the project. The idea of hundred-day initiatives was dismissed as a Band-Aid and also as unfeasible given the lack of basic capacity.

By the end of the two-day workshop, however, participants had developed some willingness to experiment with a few hundred-day initiatives, each aimed at one area of strategic importance for the agricultural sector such as pig farming, dairy production, and corn feed development. One senior-level person was designated as a strategic leader for each area.

The second workshop was conducted three weeks later; it brought together five teams, each charged with developing a goal and a work plan targeting a specific area of focus. Team membership cut across institutions and, in most cases, included representatives of the targeted beneficiaries. Intense preparations took place between the two workshops, led by the strategic leaders.

By design, development agency staff played a minimal role in this second workshop. Each team developed its own goal and work plan, often venturing quite a distance from the preliminary goals scoped out by the extended leadership group at the first workshop. At the end of the two-day workshop, team members presented their goals and preliminary work plans to the core leadership team. The mood was one of excitement and empowerment. This was expressed by several participants in their closing remarks. In the words of one participant: "We are leaving this workshop with a passion to pursue the goal that our team developed."

The implementation cycle proceeded over the next hundred days with frequent reviews by the leadership group. At the end of this cycle, another workshop was conducted where the teams presented the results of their initiatives, the lessons they learned, and their ideas for scaling up these initial efforts. In one hundred days, remarkable results were achieved.[1] Here are two illustrations:

- One cooperative in the Leon municipality of Nicaragua tripled the sale of milk produced by sixty farmers by focusing on improved quality and better marketing.
- A group of thirty farmers increased pig weight by 30 percent using an enhanced, protein-enriched corn (leveraging existing technology).

But It Is Not Just About Cows and Pigs

At one level, the Nicaragua experience with rapid results was about improving the productivity of cow and pig farmers. At a more profound level, it was about a transformation in the way people in the agricultural sector work together to support goals they are committed to.

Eighteen months after this initial intervention the momentum continues, with waves of projects infusing the agricultural sector with results and enthusiasm, and releasing untapped implementation capacity. As of April 2004, forty Rapid-Results Initiatives had been completed. Here are two samples of the additional hundred-day results that were achieved:

- By increasing value-adding steps to the selling process, twenty-seven small-scale producers were able to increase the selling price of their corn, chilote, and pepián produce by 15 percent in 120 days. To scale up, the new process (which included improved packaging and labeling and better retail targeting) is being taught in fifteen rural schools in five local regions.
- In two communities, local leaders joined forces with the mayors, with civil organizations, the National Army, and the National Forest Institute to reduce illegal traffic in forest products by 60 percent. Another community took up a similar goal and achieved an 80 percent reduction in a hundred days.

Unleashing Leadership Capacity

These results—and the continued momentum—would not have been possible without committed leadership. But where does committed leadership come from? This topic is a recurring theme in the international development literature. What if the leadership was not there—could the results have been achieved? And what if the leadership commitment wanes—can the results be sustained?

Interestingly, the locus of leadership energy that made the Nicaraguan experience successful and sustainable could not have been predicted at the outset of the effort. It was clear that the head of the Nicaraguan National Institute of Technology, Noël Pallais, provided the leadership spark that ignited the initial rapid results teams, and he played a key role in injecting a continued sense of urgency for many months after the start-up. But there was no indication at the start that Pallais would play that role. In fact, he started out as a skeptic when this idea of pursuing rapid results was first introduced. Looking back, he says, "I felt, 'What is the World Bank up to now? What do they want from us again? What new idea are they thinking about that they would like to experiment in Nicaragua? We came to this workshop and we sat down and listened to these people, and we were not in a very good mood. We had a task to do in our country and we did not want to waste our time."[2]

But at some point in the process, Pallais decided to move from the sidelines and take his rightful leadership role. Here's how he describes the shift that occurred: "I think the turning point is that the human beings that were in charge were adamant in convincing the people to do it. The people that were there to organize from the Bank were really convinced and they managed to convince us and then we managed to convince ourselves that yes, we could actually do it."

So the context that was created around rapid results in Nicaragua encouraged Pallais to commit the ultimate act of leadership: to believe that results that are seemingly beyond reach will actually be achieved and to inspire others to commit themselves to achieving these results.

This emergence of leadership capacity happened at several levels. A project leader was needed for each of the projects to achieve their aims. This role was filled by people like the heads of local milk cooperatives and the regional representatives of the key agricultural institutes. For several of these people, this was a very new experience. And yet most of them rose to the challenge and demonstrated excellent team leadership skills: they ensured that all stakeholders were "on board," they set and managed team expectations, they held people accountable for their commitments, and they played an active role with the teams when their support was needed.

For example, with only twenty days left in their hundred-day initiative and only 50 percent of the planned hundred farmers committed to cooperative agreements with agricultural technical service providers, Maria Flores, the strategic leader of one of the rapid results teams, sprang into action. She challenged her team to take radical steps to close the gap. The team rented a car and went around the villages of the region with loudspeakers announcing the benefits of the program. Over the next twenty days, the gap was closed and the team exceeded their goal at the hundred-day mark.

From Victimhood to Empowerment— View from the Trenches

Beyond unleashing leadership potential, the Nicaraguan experience with rapid results demonstrated another shift that often eludes development efforts—the shift from victimhood to empowerment.

At the initial workshop described earlier, the resistance to the idea of hundred-day results goals reflected participants' lack of confidence that they could actually achieve the results. Comments like these characterized the mood:

> "We can't even communicate with each other via e-mail. Let's deal with that first before we talk about real results in one hundred days."
> "You do not understand. It takes a hundred days here to agree on a goal."
> "We are doing all we can. I am doing my part, and I am sure everyone else is doing their part. It takes time."

Contrast this mind-set with that of one of the rapid results team members, speaking at the concluding workshop and describing how he was personally influenced by this effort:

> I am the son of a cattle rancher. My father died when I was young, and I have been raising cows the way he taught me. For a long time,

other members of the cooperative and I were lucky to make ends meet with what we were able to sell. Then one day this gentleman from the Ministry's extension agency came and told me about this initiative and invited me to be a team member. I participated in the workshop where we developed our goal and plan. Then we asked a representative from the private sector dairy exporter to join the team. And one day, this engineer sitting right there in the back of the room, came to my farm and taught me how to ensure the cleanliness of the milk we produce. During the past hundred days, we tripled the milk quantity that we sell. Now we have a safety margin of cash over and above what we need. With the confidence we gained, we went to the Bank and borrowed 100,000 cordobas, collateralized with pasture land, and we will be building a pasteurizing facility. This is how this initiative impacted my well-being.

Where does empowerment come from? In the case of Nicaragua, it emerged as the right teams got into action, challenged by their peers to achieve unusual results, and committed to specific hundred-day goals that they set for themselves.

The best evidence of this spirit is the fact that when the funding ran out and the outside consultants left, the local leadership assumed full responsibility and kept the process moving.

Turning Leadership Commitment into Action in Eritrea

Given the success in the Nicaraguan experience, it was decided to replicate the process—and, it was hoped, the impact—in another country and with a grimmer context: helping Eritrea fight HIV/AIDS.

Eritrea is a country of 4.5 million people that lies between Ethiopia and the Red Sea. Dr. Saleh Meky, its Minster of Health, and the team he had assembled from his own ministry and others (including Education and Labor), were eager to get going on the country's five-year HIV/AIDS strategic plan. The team had just completed its draft plan. In normal times, the draft would be shopped around for a few months so it could be finalized, and then its various components would be parceled out to government entities so each could advance a particular segment of the plan.

But these were not normal times. Minister Meky and his colleagues had been to too many conferences where other African health officials described how HIV/AIDS had ravaged their countries. And even though the infection rate in Eritrea was in the single digits, the Eritreans did not feel they could afford to wait before acting, nor to take the risk of business-as-usual, hit-or-miss implementation.

So when the World Bank project leader responsible for the HIV/AIDS initiatives in the country, Eva Jarawan, approached the minister with the idea of using Rapid-Results Initiatives to jump-start and fuel the implementation process, he was willing to listen.

Getting Started—Achieving Unlikely Results in the First Hundred Days

The first conversation with the minister about the idea of rapid results took place in late February 2003. In March, with help from Jarawan and her consulting team, six rapid results teams were launched in the Central Region of Eritrea. Each team set a truly ambitious goal—a result that would achieve a significant gain on one priority theme in the five-year strategic plan. And each goal had to be achieved in one hundred days or less.

One of the initiatives, for example, focused on increasing the use of Voluntary Counseling and Testing Services—referred to as VCT. The hundred-day goal: *"During the last 2 weeks of June 2003, achieve a 25% increase in the number of users of VCT services, with the first week in March 2003 as a benchmark, and get user satisfaction rating above 80%, measured through user surveys."*

One hundred days later, the weekly number of clients had ramped up by *80 percent,* from 220 in early March to 390 in the last week of June! The trend line moved steadily upward (except for the Lent and Easter period), and continued to rise beyond the initial hundred days. Moreover, user exit questionnaires (developed as part of the VCT Rapid-Results Initiative) showed a consistent 95 percent level of satisfaction with the quality of the VCT service.

To achieve their initial goal, the rapid results team opened three new VCT sites, trained five additional counselors, distributed Rapid Test kits, procured some new equipment and furniture (videos for waiting rooms, for example), and put in place a systematic tracking and monitoring system—accomplishments the team confessed they would never have thought possible when they embarked on this effort.

VCT was only one of the results areas that were tackled in the initial wave of rapid-cycle initiatives in Asmara, the capital of Eritrea. Other rapid results teams delivered equally impressive results. Here are few illustrations:

- The Orthodox and Catholic Churches each started a new home-based care program in Asmara staffed by trained volunteers, with a total of 117 families receiving care at the hundred-day mark (exceeding their goal of 100), while the Evangelical Church added a nutritional care component to its ongoing home-based care program.
- Of the hundred commercial sex workers who participated in the hundred-day peer support program, seventy-two have become regular users of female condoms (exceeding their 50 percent goal), and thirty-four have started using VCT services (somewhat under the 50 percent goal).
- A school-based HIV/AIDS prevention program was started in six schools, focused on delaying the onset of sexual activity among young people and increasing the percentage of condom users among sexually active students. The data suggests that this effort actually influenced student behaviors within one hundred days, and it has fueled a rapid ramp-up of school-based prevention activities country-wide.

Beyond the Initial Results: Scaling Up

Despite the initial indicators of success in Asmara, Minister Meky and Dr. Anderhen Tesfazion (his national HIV/AIDS director) preferred to wait before signaling their intent to scale up the effort. All the teams, along with most of the stakeholder group that participated in the initial workshop in March, met for a two-day workshop at the end of the hundred-day period. Each team described what they had set out to do, what they actually accomplished, what they learned. They also outlined their initial ideas for what needed to be done to scale up the initial impact by at least a factor of five.

The results that were achieved and the enthusiasm that was expressed at the wrap-up workshop convinced the Minister and Dr. Tesfazion that the Rapid-Results Initiative needed to be deepened in the Central Region and broadened to other regions.

In the Central Region, scaling up took different forms for each of the areas of focus.

Voluntary Counseling and Testing: Shifting the Focus to Tackle New Challenges

After the first VCT initiative was completed, Dr. Musfin Worede, the regional medical director, and his team decided to shift their VCT focus from the downtown district of Asmara to the suburbs.

There they challenged new teams to pursue different, more ambitious goals for expanding the use of VCT. Three teams were launched simultaneously; each focused on one of the Asmara suburbs, in partnership with youth clubs. The same discipline was followed. Local teams were challenged to set hundred-day stretch goals. They were empowered to develop their own plans to achieve these goals and were supported through centrally managed resources.

The third wave of VCT Rapid-Results Initiatives shifted the focus still further, from increasing utilization of VCT services to reducing transmission risks. Hundred-day goals were established—each aimed at increasing enrollment in post-test clubs in each VCT Center.

As a result of these efforts, Dr. Worede increased the annual goal for VCT use in Asmara from twelve thousand to fifteen thousand users, and by December, the actual number of users was just shy of twenty thousand!

Two-Way Learning: Behavior Change
Among Commercial Sex Workers

The rapid results effort involving commercial sex workers offered insights into another aspect of implementation acceleration: Where does the knowledge for change reside? And how do we tap into this knowledge? In the case of the commercial sex workers (CSWs), Johannes Malaki, a director at the Ministry of Labor, prepared for a scale-up workshop where five CSW teams were launched simultaneously, each taking on a hundred-day goal that involved working with eighty of their peers to achieve anywhere from 40 to 70 percent adoption rates of female condoms and use of VCT centers. The five CSW team leaders helped design the workshop, identifying key issues and challenges that they wanted to discuss at the workshop before their teams set their goals and developed their plans. The team leaders insisted that some of their clients participate in the workshop, as the issues and challenges often involved clients.

The workshop was an eye-opener for those from the Ministries of Labor and of Health. New issues were put on the table by the CSWs. For example:

> *"How do we ensure that we use female condoms when we, or our clients, are drunk?"*

> *"How do we handle our protectors [pimps] when they insist that we practice unsafe sex with clients because they get a premium price for this?"*

Since the workshop was codesigned by the commercial sex workers themselves, it was an opportunity for an honest dialogue between them and government officials about the difficulties CSWs encounter implementing safe sex behaviors that they hear about in the typical public health awareness–building campaigns.

One of the strategies developed by the CSWs for dealing with drunk clients, for example, was to create support groups—so they could help each other handle these situations. A few weeks after the launch workshop a drunk client insisted on having unprotected sex with one of the CSWs in the rapid results teams. The CSW called out for her support group of two colleagues, who helped her overpower the man. They all ended up in the police station. The CSW called Malaki and explained the situation. He joined them in the police station and argued with the police officer that the CSWs were acting in self-defense as they overpowered the client—that having unprotected sex is a life-threatening act. His argument won the day, and the CSWs were released while the drunk client spent the night in jail![3]

Malaki captured the essence of the shift that was taking place: "This is new for us, and it is important for us. We've met with CSWs before, but it's always been one-way communications, with us teaching them. This is much better. They are teaching us and themselves. And we see that they know a lot."

The CSW teams set higher goals, in the aggregate, than what Malaki was aiming for. And over the next hundred days they exceeded their goals. In June 2004, Malaki was preparing to launch the third wave of initiatives, targeting a thousand CSWs in the Central Region.

A Study in Contrasts: School-Based Prevention Program—Before and After

The school-based prevention team decided on a wide-scale rollout of the activities they had initiated in their first Rapid-Results Initiative. In each of six schools about one hundred younger and one hundred older children were identified. Behavior change goals were established, and a number of activities were set in motion to drive this behavior change, such as awareness workshops, peer group meetings, sessions with parents, teachers, and students, extracurricular clubs, debate and theater activities, all emphasizing the importance of delaying sexual activity for the younger cohort and of safe sex for the older.

Here's how the impact of their work was reported on by Don Bundy, World Bank education specialist who visited Asmara about eight months after the first wave of Rapid-Results Initiatives was completed: "The

Eritrea Ministry of Education had made much progress in strategy, policy, national curriculum and school health programming—but little on actually promoting positive behavior in schools. But ten months after the Rapid-Results Initiatives were launched, I found that a school-wide peer education program, based on best practice and absorbing the teacher trainers, was in place in all secondary schools and half the primary schools in Central Province. This was supported by school environmental improvements, aimed at retaining girls in schools and promoting socialization of youth (such as gender separate latrines and basic sports facilities)."[4]

Bundy cited a pre- and postevaluation of reported behaviors that indicated a reduction in sexual activity from 9 percent to 2 percent among the targeted cohort. While such figures are not reliable, a reduction in reported activity is now interpreted as evidence of increased recognition of risk. Two out of the remaining four provinces have now implemented similar programs, using Rapid-Results Initiatives. Bundy adds, "What is interesting is that the success in the Central Province automatically triggered demand in other provinces—and with a little support from the pioneering teams, other provinces were able to catch up with the Central Province in terms of performance."

Bundy pointed out that none of the cast of characters had changed from the period before the rapid results approach was introduced. And the same financial resources (donor funds) were available both before and after. In fact, for several years funds available to the Ministry of Education for similar work had been largely untapped. But within a span of eight months the use of financial support increased by 300 percent. The very same people were tapping into available resources and expertise and achieving very different results.

Spreading the Antivirus of Rapid Results

In October 2003, Minister Meky challenged other regional medical directors to get a similar process under way in their regions—starting with the Northern Red Sea. Local coaches from all regions were trained, and they participated in the launch of the process in Massawa, the main port city of Eritrea. Priority areas were identified, and hundred-day rapid results teams were launched. The teams faced several difficulties, including slow disbursement. Nevertheless, they were able to achieve impressive results. For example, the use of VCT increased from an average of 50 per month in October 2003 to an average of 120 per month in January 2004 (exceeding their 75 percent increase goal). The use of VCT continued to rise beyond the hundred-day initiatives, and it had reached 170 per month in March.

In February 2004, the Debub Region followed suit. This time, though, the process was orchestrated entirely by local coaches, with guidance from Dr. Anderhen Tesfazion, the national HIV/AIDS director, and support from the medical directors and others who had spearheaded the rapid results work in Massawa and Asmara. In May 2004, the third region, Ansaba, got initiated into the process. And in June 2004, the Gashbarka Region began.

Meanwhile, Dr. Worede of the Central Region continues to drive results in Asmara: "This is now a way of working for us: when we have a challenge to overcome, we attack it with a rapid results team."

It is too early to tell if the process will continue to transform the way work on HIV/AIDS gets accomplished. No doubt there is much more work that needs to be done by Minister Meky and his team to permanently embed the process in the way the programs are managed. But the signs are encouraging.

Migration Across National Boundaries

The success of the Eritrea experience with rapid results has sparked interest among other African leaders. The message is compelling: it is possible to get results if you actually focus on achieving results. By June 2004, Kenya, Sierra Leone, and Mozambique had each begun to adopt the approach as a way to accelerate implementation of their health and other development efforts. The World Bank is providing overall sponsorship for this shift.

In Mozambique, the focus of the rapid results work is HIV/AIDS. The National AIDS Control Council launched eleven initiatives in May 2004.

In Sierra Leone, Rapid Results Initiatives are being used to accelerate implementation of HIV/AIDS programs, and also to help newly elected local councils deliver results to their communities. In one area, for example, the initial goal was to achieve three thousand visits to the local voluntary counseling and testing centers by the end of a hundred days. Long before the end of the hundred-day period, they began to experience more than two thousand visits a week! The local council work started in June 2004, and it has yielded a number of initiatives focused on local priorities, such as sewage cleanup, garbage collection, and revenue generation.

In Kenya, the work has been under way since March 2003, and it is touching a number of sectors that have been identified as critical for the country's economic recovery. During the first year, Rapid Results Initiatives were launched in HIV/AIDS, Tourism, Security, Water, and Agriculture. Some of the goals that were set by the rapid results teams are shown in Table 9.1.

The Sustainability Challenge

Recognizing the implementation weakness in past programs, the professionals who provide development assistance are increasingly focusing on what they're calling "results-on-the-ground." Without doubt, the goals that the rapid results teams in Nicaragua, Eritrea, Kenya, Mozambique, Sierra Leone, and elsewhere are pursuing are aimed at results-on-the-ground. But achieving these immediate goals needs to be a leading indicator of a more profound aspiration: enhancing the capacity in these countries for making change happen. In every project new skills and new management disciplines are being developed in both sponsors

Table 9.1   Rapid Results Initiatives Launched in Kenya, June 2004: Sample Goals of Teams in HIV/AIDS and Water

HIV/AIDS

Team	Goal
Young Women's Prevention	Increase the number of young women visiting Voluntary Counseling and Testing centers in the Mukuru area of Nairobi from 100/month to 1200/month by October, 2004.
Orphans and Vulnerable Children	By October 15, upgrade the level of support and care provided to OVCs in primary schools in Mukuru area to achieve 80 percent satisfaction among OVCs that they receive better support than at the beginning of the hundred days.
Workplace Prevention	Establish a community center with VCT services and achieve 25 percent VCT usage among Jua Kali workers in Emtakasi area by October 1.

WATER

Team	Goal
Water Supply— Nakuru	Ensure an average of six hours/day of water supply for eight zones in Nakuru in the next 120 days (by October 15) (to be further refined with the team).
Irrigation	Ensure that by November 30, 2004, at least 80 percent of the beneficiaries in Elengata Enterit will have water and will be irrigating at least one hectare each.
Administration— Accounts	Reduce the time taken for voucher preparation to payment from an average time of one week to two days for internal clients and from one month to four days for external clients.

and participants. Moreover, the "how" of the rapid results approach provides a vehicle for strengthening three critical capacity levers:

- Capacity of leaders to challenge and to motivate
- Local empowerment and accountability
- Capacity for cross-institutional collaboration

Capacity to Challenge and Motivate

By breaking results down to hundred-day building blocks, senior people in government at various levels can practice the art of challenging and motivating teams to achieve superior results. The scope is focused and time-bound, and the leaders get the coaching and coaxing to help step into a new role—to make the shift from government bureaucrat to inspiring and demanding leader. In fact, each initiative has a "strategic leader" whose role is to challenge and motivate the team. This becomes a hands-on developmental opportunity for government officials. Enhancing and unleashing this capacity is one of the levers that makes it possible to sustain and expand the initial results.

Empowerment and Accountability

People respond to a challenge—particularly when the challenge involves a real impact on their lives. The Rapid-Results Initiatives are mechanisms for challenging people to take accountability for results that affect their own well-being.

For example, typical behavior change programs among commercial sex workers are designed by training and communication experts and delivered in workshops. The rapid results approach reverses the roles. The CSW rapid results teams in Eritrea were made up of commercial sex workers themselves: they set their goals and developed their plans, and they reached out to the center and to the experts to help them deliver on their goal. So people who are being helped are empowered to set their own goals and find their own solutions.

Cross-Institutional Collaboration

Worthwhile results rarely come neatly aligned with governmental units. Rather, they require the collaboration of multiple players in diverse institutions, often spanning several sectors. This was certainly the case for HIV/AIDS in Eritrea. Several government institutions, including the Ministries of Health, Labor, and Education, needed to join forces with each other and with religious groups as well as private citizen groups including the organization representing people living with HIV/AIDS and various youth associations. By focusing on a single result that they feel jointly accountable for, people from different organizations are able to transcend some of the typical organizational turf issues.

These levers are as much about attitudes as they are about process and skills. Rapid results projects thrust people into situations where they need to act in new ways. This personal transformation is what makes all other changes possible, and it is the prerequisite for sustaining the results and institutionalizing the process.

Results Beget Capacity . . . and Capacity Begets Results

The hundred-day implementation cycle of the rapid results undertakings provides fast and frequent opportunities for reinforcing the necessary attitudes, skills, and behaviors. With each wave of initiatives confidence is built at the leadership and the local levels. Thus, with each cycle of results achievement, capacity for implementation and for change is strengthened.

Each of the rapid results stories outlined in this chapter is a work in progress. Much more experience is needed to refine the approach and to ensure that it is able to support progress against some of the toughest challenges imaginable.

As the work moves forward it is important that it be done in an experimental, empirical fashion. As emphasized in Chapter Six, the quest should not be for the universal model—that's a futile endeavor. Unique strategies and tactics for successfully tackling development challenges will undoubtedly have to be uncovered and molded by the leadership groups in each country—through engaging and empowering stakeholders at all levels and unleashing their creativity and capacity to make change happen. The experiences of Nicaragua, Eritrea, Kenya, and other countries shed light on how Rapid-Results Initiatives can be used by committed leaders to accomplish this.

Chapter Ten describes how rapid results projects can be the catalysts for powerful strategic planning—for countries, for companies, and for enterprises of every kind.

Key Points

- For more than sixty years international agencies have tried to help the developing nations of the world free themselves of poverty—with far too little success.

- Success was limited in large part because the methods usually were of the big-fix kind, and countries lacked the grassroots implementation capability to make the big programs succeed.

- Developmental goals in public health, education, agriculture, and economics can all be attacked via rapid results projects—which produce immediate results and build implementation capability.

- You don't need outside experts to run the programs— local leaders can do it.

- Through these initiatives, the "target population" ceases to be a target and becomes the driver for change.

10

SPARK STRATEGIC MOMENTUM WITH RAPID RESULTS

Thus far we have discussed the way rapid results projects can accelerate progress on strategic issues: a rapid results project is a powerful implementation tool for aligning organizational resources and for speeding progress toward key objectives. But the power of rapid results goes beyond the effective implementation of strategy. These projects can, in fact, open a new approach to strategic planning itself and how it can contribute to progress.

The basic idea is that rapid-cycle projects provide a mechanism for integrating strategic planning into the life of the organization and positioning it as the driver of success. This can happen through two important shifts:

- Instead of the common experience of strategic planning as an annual distraction, it becomes an ongoing, iterative process.
- Instead of a small group of people completing the planning assignment in isolation, the entire organization becomes involved in the evolution of strategy.

Through the consistent application of rapid results projects, strategy development can be framed in a new way, as an iterative, participatory process whereby the entire organization is engaged in creating, implementing, and evolving strategy. The value of the output increases as cycles of planning and action sharpen the strategic focus. As Henry Mintzberg wrote in his *Harvard Business*

KEITH E. MICHAELSON, lead author; Thomas Leder provided case material.

Review article "Crafting Strategy": "Formulation and implementation merge into a fluid process of learning through which creative strategies evolve."[1]

The Trap of Linear Strategic Planning

The aim of most strategic planning is to march in a fairly disciplined way toward the creation of a big conceptual picture of what the organization should be in the future. Unfortunately, the process is often quite disconnected from the realities of the business—as viewed by the people operating it—and is seen as a time-devouring activity that leads nowhere.

Professional corporate planners often find themselves in a virtually impossible position: doing their work in relative isolation from the rest of the organization and following a sequential, linear model in which they deliver a fully formulated strategy for implementation. Typically, the professional planners are asked to perform some variation of these four steps:

1. Evaluate the current situation through a SWOT analysis, that is, mapping organizational strengths, weaknesses, opportunities, and threats.
2. Formulate strategic objectives—a vision of the future.
3. Develop a set of strategic issues that must be tackled to move forward.
4. Deliver the strategic issues and work with each business or department to develop the steps required to carry out the strategic plan.

Through this intellectual exercise, a set of one-year goals keyed to the achievement of future strategic objectives is established. But the output is speculation, at best; the environment is changing rapidly, and the plans are not embedded in a process structured to test their validity against both the real-time opportunities and the obstacles to achieving the goals.

Meanwhile, for the people at the divisional level, the yearly planning process becomes a dreary bureaucratic chore; they cannot wait to complete their planning responsibilities and get back to work. Absolved by the corporate process from doing thoughtful planning connected to their own business, their time is spent on establishing budget targets and planning how to meet them rather than on recognizing and assessing new challenges. The disconnection of strategy from the real needs and current capabilities of the business means that the odds of generating commitment to implementation can be very low. Even the most energetic of planners lose heart over time as immediate priorities take precedence over their strategic vision and they are unable to exert influence over the people who must carry out their plans.

Despite repeated frustrations and the recognition that much of the work fails to pay off, this cycle of activity is repeated year after year. Tradition demands it; businesses are expected to have strategic plans. Investors and analysts require planning as a sign that management is doing its job and as a guide to making their own decisions. In fact, most senior managers insist that setting strategic directions is one of their most critical responsibilities. Corporate planning departments invest in the development of detailed planning models and processes. Their assumption seems to be that with the right processes in place and the right data fed in, a strategy will somehow emerge. Yet a great many people in business, including those who must play critical roles in the formulation and implementation of directions, have long ago stopped expecting much to come of all this effort. They have ceded responsibility for creating the future so they can get on with managing their day-to-day business.

Rapid Results Projects Shift the Paradigm

Through a strategic planning process that integrates intellectual direction-setting with action-oriented rapid results projects, an organization can, over time, blend strategic ambitions and realistic expectations. People can balance the fantastic and the feasible—and create a working environment in which no one settles for business-as-usual and everyone takes a keen interest in reaching strategic goals. This requires the adoption of a planning paradigm that is *developmental*, meaning that planning is not just about defining objectives and creating plans but is also focused on building mastery in all the areas where progress is necessary to gain control over the future of the enterprise. The developmental approach meshes planning with action to accomplish new objectives with the available organizational resources. As described in earlier chapters, managers begin by focusing on the accomplishment of urgent but relatively straightforward goals. They use the planning disciplines to achieve those goals; then they exploit the skills, abilities, and confidence developed by these early projects to identify and tackle more complex and more far-reaching goals. Thus strategic planning begins not with the remote but with the immediate, and results achievement becomes a critical input to the further development of strategy. This also is a way of overcoming the rigidity of many corporate strategies. Rapid results projects can help with experimentation and innovation in different market segments simultaneously—in what Gary Hamel and Liisa Välikangas call "stratlets" in their article "Quest for Resilience."[2]

This chapter illustrates these ideas with examples from three organizations that have achieved a remarkable step-up in performance through a shift in their approach to planning: Public Service of New Hampshire (PSNH), a public electric utility; Deutsche Gesellschaft fuer Technische Zusammenarbeit (GTZ), a German government-sponsored organization that provides aid for developing countries; and the Retail Marketing function of Fidelity Investments.

An Electric Utility Faces an Uncertain Future

In the year 2000, Public Service of New Hampshire was a prime example of a company where the yearly planning process had become disconnected from the needs of the business. The primary electric utility for the state and an operating subsidiary of the Northeast Utilities System, the company needed to reposition itself in a rapidly changing electrical industry environment. Its planning process offered little help. As Ian Wilson, head of Corporate Communications, explains, "We had forms to fill out detailing dozens of goals and objectives. The main out-come of business planning was check-the-box responsibilities related to operational and financial commitments rather than an aspirational vision and strategy. Our real focus throughout the year continued to be on the particular crisis of the moment." Bob Hybsch, director of Customer Operations, adds, "We created a fifty-page plan, handed it in, and hoped one or two positive things would come out of it. It wasn't embraced by the business, and little was done to relate the plan to our work during the year."

In recent years, PSNH had come a long way in improving its cus-tomer service and its key relationships with state regulators, but it was still caught in a cycle of reacting to its environment. At the end of 2000, Gary Long, the new president, and Kevin Walker, then vice president of operations, recognized that emerging industry trends meant that the future of the business hung in the balance. The fate of the company would be determined by what was accomplished in the next several years. They decided that the time had come to sponsor a new approach to planning.

At that time, two critical issues had to be tackled:

- The need to increase earnings in the regulated utility business environment.
- The need to decide whether PSNH would divest its power genera-tion facilities or continue to own and operate them. The trend being set as deregulation swept the electric utility industry across the United States was for divestiture of generation.

At an initial strategic planning session in November 2000, Gary Long presented the two critical issues to a group of twenty-five senior man-agers and asked them to think about how to get moving on both issues. The planning session did not, at this early stage, elicit fundamentally new concepts. Its aim was to get focused and get started. It yielded these outcomes:

On increasing earnings: From a long list of ideas, the senior group narrowed the focus down to four key priorities to be tackled first: distribution efficiency, new products and services, customer retention, and outage recovery.

On generation: The initial focus was confined to doing an analysis of the alternatives for the future of the generation assets and formulating a position on their future in consultation with the regulators.

From previous experience as a power plant manager and as head of Steam Distribution for Con Edison in New York City, Kevin Walker brought firsthand experience with rapid results projects. He knew they had the potential to create the essential momentum. With his guidance, champions for each priority were selected whose job was to define a specific rapid results project, select the team, and set the project in motion.

A new pathway for strategy formulation was evolving. Instead of a report created by a small planning team, with lists of objectives and tasks for each functional area, the immediate product was an agreement on urgent priorities and the assignment of clear accountability for action. Rather than managing purely functional activities, the senior managers charged cross-functional teams with the responsibility of producing tangible results over the next hundred days.

Engaging the Organization in an Iterative Learning Process

In retrospect, the goals the teams set for the initial projects to increase earnings don't seem all that ambitious, but they did pose significant challenges for the teams and they provided an appropriate starting point for evolving a developmental strategy.

For example, one project focused on local outage recovery. This team's goal was to reduce by 50 percent the time that it took to restore service after an electrical outage. Every aspect of the process was up for scrutiny, and one critical discovery about the system for generating the "trouble tickets"—the documents that directed crews to the location of an outage—soon emerged. While everyone had been waiting for years for a planned new system to resolve frustrating shortcomings, the team discovered that the process could be improved with the current system through some immediate upgrades. A second project focused on making sure that when a line crew arrived to do a job, the site would be ready for them to get to work, thus eliminating costly wasted trips. Two of fourteen work centers were selected to participate in the initial rapid results project. A third project began to explore what new products and services could be introduced within the regulated business environment, and a fourth focused on bringing back customers who had left the PSNH system in favor of self-generation.

Each of the four project teams set specific, measurable goals to be achieved by the end of three months; and virtually all those goals were achieved.

Upon completion of this first round of earnings-oriented projects, each was summarized, and recommendations were made for sustaining progress. The experience had led to a number of new insights about obstacles to improvement. Gary Long, for example, shared his learning about trouble tickets: "To deal with this issue, it took ten years for us to complain about the problems and then three months to solve them when we put our minds to it."

An unspoken assumption of the top managers had been that once the first projects proved successful, people would be eager to expand the approach to other business challenges. But the culture of PSNH was not yet ready to plunge into an ambitious change process. People who had not been involved in the team projects were not particularly enthusiastic about adopting the innovations. Even among some senior people there was a feeling that rapid results projects, while interesting, were taking too much time and effort away from daily work.

Refining the Strategic Focus

Despite this lingering resistance, the initial projects were successful enough that senior management decided to push forward with a new round of projects. In preparation for launching the next round, Long and Walker established a clear leadership framework. Co-champions for each of the priorities were identified. In addition to launching and supporting a results-achieving team, their role was to drive progress on the overall strategic priority. This meant that they had to set year-end objectives for the business results they would deliver. And they also had to identify a portfolio of issues to become the focus of rapid results projects. The entire champion group began to meet every six weeks to review their plans and the action under way. In this way the overall strategy became the shared agenda for a group of leaders from across the business. This was a dramatic shift for a business that had traditionally operated within rigid functional silos.

In the following months, under the leadership of the project champions across all the functions, rapid results projects that focused on all strategic priorities were launched. The mutual reinforcement of results achievement and strategy formulation can best be illustrated by reviewing the streams of work in just one of the strategic priorities—distribution efficiencies.

Electric Distribution: Operational Gains Lead to Strategic Decision Making

Two of the initial projects (job-site readiness and outage recovery) had focused on improving performance in electric distribution. Building on these early successes, co-champions Bob Hybsch and John Libby, the directors of Customer Operations and Energy Delivery, targeted more ambitious performance issues that had broader strategic links. They launched projects to increase the productivity of the line maintenance crews, to improve the management of the materials inventory, and to streamline the process aimed at reducing damage to electric lines from falling tree limbs.

The net impact of these projects was significant improvement in system reliability—as measured by the average number of minutes PSNH customers are without power during the year. As this reliability effort moved forward, it shifted away from focusing on individual issues one at a time. The distribution efficiency champions developed and acted upon a holistic view of a high-performance distribution system under the leadership of a senior engineer who was proposing changes in the company's fundamental approach to system design. As design changes were implemented and substations were reconfigured, the reliability numbers continued to improve.

The enhanced operational performance and the improved external relationships the company had achieved were not missed by regulators, who watched with growing interest as the company demonstrated increasing skill and confidence in managing the state's electrical resources. State officials and regulators, faced with a difficult legal and regulatory dilemma with another New Hampshire utility, decided that an acquisition of that troubled utility would be the best strategy. They were confident that PSNH could provide the solution. This opportunity fit nicely with the emerging view of PSNH growth objectives, based on a new sense of confidence and potential. Although its leaders had never made an acquisition before, they formed a team to carry out an effective purchase and integration process.

Commenting on their growing capacity to respond flexibly to strategic opportunity, Bob Hybsch says, "I have learned that strategy is iterative, that it is continually developing. You have to be flexible enough to take a hard rudder right and head in a new direction when an opportunity comes up."

Power Generation: Strategic Decision Making Links to Operational Gains

While the earnings improvement projects were being carried out, a parallel effort was under way on the strategic issue of divesting the company's power generation assets. The starting assumption for these studies had been that PSNH would divest its generation facilities in line with the industry-wide trend. But a number of discussions held with state lawmakers during this period revealed that they had not yet made firm decisions about the future. In fact, as their studies were carried out, legislative and regulatory sentiment started to shift.

They were increasingly impressed by the fact that the rush to divestiture of generation assets by utilities around the United States was leading to many unfortunate outcomes—the worst being the notorious energy shortages experienced in California just two years previously. The performance and reliability improvements being demonstrated by PSNH—and the company's ability to absorb the troubled company— added impetus to their shifting views.

As the decision time approached, the managers of PSNH's gener- ation business took some steps to generate immediate income: the power market had recently become so volatile that prices could fluc- tuate radically in a matter of hours. Taking an entrepreneurial stance, PSNH's power dispatchers and generating stations teamed up on a series of rapid-cycle projects to ensure that they would be available to deliver power when prices were peaking. The ability to manage availability against market demand realized millions of dollars in rev- enue, most of which would, over time, be passed along to customers in the form of rate reductions. These efforts fundamentally changed the economics that would determine the decisions on the future of the business.

With the earnings from this tour de force combined with all the other progress shown by the company, the regulators were comfort- able reaching the decision that PSNH should retain its generation assets. With that issue resolved, the co-champions of the generation strategic work targeted additional operational improvements. Rapid results projects were launched to reduce the cost of power plant maintenance and to improve operating efficiencies. In addition, they began to look for strategic moves that could contribute to growth. They gained approval to build a renewable energy generating station and began exploration into the use of alternative energy sources such as wind farms.

Electric Distribution had begun with operations improvement and blended it quickly with strategic planning; Generation went the other way, starting with strategic planning and moving quickly to include operational improvement. And now the two major parts of

Figure 10.1   Comparing Strategic Horizons

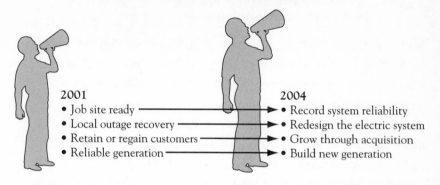

2001
- Job site ready
- Local outage recovery
- Retain or regain customers
- Reliable generation

2004
- Record system reliability
- Redesign the electric system
- Grow through acquisition
- Build new generation

the business had transformed themselves in three years. As illustrated in Figure 10.1, when the process began, they had been virtually 100 percent preoccupied with day-to-day pressures. They now were advancing simultaneously on both operations improvement and strategic growth—and grasping how the close iterative link between strategy and action reinforced the power of each.

With a solid foundation of improved performance, a new vision began to emerge, that of a company able to use its strengths to manage entrepreneurial growth even within the boundaries of its regulated business environment. Operations Support manager Terry Large conveys the essence of that transformation: "We have unlocked many more minds. We have gone from having one or two strategic leaders to having twenty or thirty. The most critical shift we have made is to give hundreds of people the opportunity to contribute to strategic thinking in our rapid-cycle projects and Work-Outs."

President Gary Long summarizes his perspective: "Success has pushed out our strategic horizon. As we have empowered people to set directions and get results, they have developed a new level of self-confidence. I now have a large group of what I think of as my 'partners in strategy' who are continually testing more ideas than I could ever come up with myself."

Developmental Strategic Planning
in an International Aid Service Provider

Deutsche Gesellschaft für Technische Zusammenarbeit provides development aid services to improve living conditions in developing countries. With ninety-five hundred employees in sixty-seven country offices, GTZ is currently funded chiefly by one German federal ministry. But in the future a growing portion of its services will be commissioned by international financial institutions and nongovernment organizations, or will be developed in partnerships with private industry.

GTZ senior management recognized that diminishing government resources, tougher competition for international funds, and clients who were demanding more integrated services with higher impact all raised fundamental questions about the future of the organization: Which new market segments should they serve and what new service offerings should they build? Applying its traditional approach to strategy development, GTZ would identify potential market segments, formulate a strategy for each segment, select the most attractive opportunities from the portfolio, and build a consolidated set of plans to develop competitive advantage. Only then would they actually get into action. It would be a tremendous up-front task and one not at all certain of success.

Christoph Beier, co-head of the Planning and Development Department, which coordinates GTZ's twenty-seven hundred projects, wanted to test a method that was more rapid and more certain of success. One option was to implement the traditional planning process, but in a fast-track mode; get it done, and push the goals down the line. It was clear to the Planning and Development Department heads, however, that top-down plans would not generate the action necessary to achieve success. A second option was to structure the organization into specific business areas and have each of them do its own planning. But how could they determine which units to form? The structure had to follow the strategy. And a lengthy process of restructuring could diminish the energy level of the whole organization.

Christoph Beier and his colleague, Cornelia Richter, proposed a third pathway: some specific, obviously important, new service opportunities would be selected as the immediate strategic priorities, and teams would aim for results and learning in those areas within a few months. GTZ would get moving quickly and avoid lengthy up-front planning and cumbersome organizational redesign. After discussing the alternatives, the senior management committee approved the proposal.

Four of the senior managers, with the heads of Planning and Development, formed a leadership group. Each member of this group recruited a team and assigned them an overall business challenge that they then had to turn into a rapid results project. Each project was to achieve position-building business results within five to eight months—a revolutionary time frame for an organization used to a very long-term perspective. And each project had to demonstrate the potential for sustainable competitive advantage in a new business segment.

As they got under way, all the teams had to come up with innovative offerings. For example, one of them developed a new offering called "Rehabilitation and Crisis Prevention," a recovery process for countries suffering from intrastate wars. The idea was to integrate the emergency aid that provides food and shelter with processes for strengthening local government and building employment and security. This groundbreaking approach would provide a faster and significantly greater contribution to the lives of suffering populations than the traditional emergency aid alone. The team conceived the offering and set a goal to receive an actual assignment of €5 million. If successful, GTZ would be the first in this service area with an integrated cross-product aid program.

Another team focused on a service for rural areas in Latin America to reduce the risks of weather-related disasters. The idea was to build a collaboration of financial institutions, national governments, and reinsurers to induce farmers to adopt a more risk-averse way of farming in these areas. The goal was to reach agreement with these organizations on a pilot project to model how to prevent disasters in rural areas—and open an opportunity for GTZ to be a market leader.

From Short-Term Success to Long-Term Direction

The Rehabilitation and Crisis Prevention team won €4.5 million from donors. The weather disaster prevention team won acceptance for their concept and were awarded new contracts worth €2.5 million in two countries. Another project secured a contract for a water utility in Asia in a build-operate partnership, a completely new field of activity for GTZ. Proposals for new GTZ AIDS programs were under negotiation with donors. An e-learning service started a partnership with a big software firm; and negotiations were begun to implement vocational training in a Central African state. GTZ thus established a presence in five new markets essential for the positioning of the whole enterprise.

Here was a quite new way to formulate strategy. It focused on achieving specific competitive advantages to win contracts and to build sustained positions in target service areas. Each rapid-cycle project delivered a specific business result as well as insight into the longer-term strategic priority. In a critical shift in role, the strategic planners became business leaders who were committed to the achievement of near-term results as well as to longer-term strategies.

The examples set by the initial rapid results projects began to spill over into the regular planning process in functional units. Using the new methodology, other parts of the Planning and Development Department and also the regional offices have begun to formulate business strategies driven by rapid results goals and plans within a bottom-up process. Thus a new planning approach is being introduced—without a big formal procedure. A rapid results orientation is slowly becoming a benchmark for the GTZ way of planning. The process of defining, attacking, and winning over new market segments is now becoming a part of corporate thinking and strategic behavior.

What began as a strategy process has now become a major transformation process.

A New Paradigm for Strategic Planning

The PSNH and GTZ stories show that it is possible to move from a rigid, linear planning process that has become focused primarily on control to a flexible process that is focused primarily on experimentation and learning (see Table 10.1). Through the application of rapid-cycle projects the balance shifts from analytic work to near-term action. And success in the action sharpens the analytic work. Results become the vehicle for the evolving of strategy.

A Quick Aside: No Strategic Secrets?

Many strategic planners worry that with widespread involvement in planning, a company will not be able to carry out strategic moves that need to be kept confidential. Exploration of an acquisition is an example. But nothing in this methodology prevents a company from carrying out a confidential exploration even when the entire organization is engaged in action and planning activities. Moreover, as a company becomes more effective in achieving its aims, secrecy will be less important. Toyota is a prime illustration. Confident that others can never have the agility to match its perpetual, dynamic innovation, the company maintains an open-door policy. Anyone can inspect Toyota's greatest "secret," its manufacturing operations.

**Table 10.1   Strategic Planning: From Linear Mode
to Developmental Mode**

From	To
Planning as preparation for action	Iterative cycles of planning and action
Yearly event	Ongoing process
Centrally controlled	Entrepreneurial leadership with central direction
Intellectual process	Action-learning process
Limited involvement	Entire organization involved
Closed-door process with limited communications	Process transparent and understood by everyone

Introducing Strategic Planning into a Customer-Transaction-Driven Business

A number of years ago, Roger Servison headed the Retail Marketing organization at Fidelity Investments. Although the company was the largest provider of mutual funds, it had grown in volume but not in market share in a growing industry. To be more competitive and win greater share, Servison began a process of transformation across the retail side of Fidelity.

The greatest obstacle to growth, he recognized, was rooted in the very strategy and structure that had been keys to Fidelity's success: as Fidelity grew, each product line operated as an independent, entrepreneurial entity, seeking out its own customers and serving them in its own ways. While this fueled tremendous growth, it also forced individual investors to do their own integration of Fidelity's many products. Customers had to construct their own portfolio strategies and deal with a vast array of service representatives and contact points—all the while being solicited for business by other Fidelity units. Many customers were being overwhelmed and frustrated. Moreover, many of them lacked the sophistication to develop their own integrated investment strategies.

Servison met with his peers who ran the various parts of the retail business and with his own product managers. Together they formulated a vision for a more integrated retail business and developed a bold set of aspirations for market share growth—both of which they communicated to the entire retail organization.

The problem was that the retail organization did not have a process for translating the market share aspirations and integrated business vision into reality. Yes, people were feeling committed and they knew they needed to do things differently, but it wasn't clear to them how to proceed.

A Results Focus Drives Strategic Thinking

To break the logjam, Servison had to create his own unique mini-architecture for change. He decided to initiate a series of cross-organizational project teams, each aimed at achieving a hundred-day rapid result related to the overall market share improvement goals.

Servison engaged his direct reports and a number of his peers in the retail parts of Fidelity to identify potential breakthrough ideas. They did some joint brainstorming and generated lists of possibilities for the initial effort. They selected the five ideas that seemed to have the most promise for both financial success and learning about how to achieve share growth. They selected a team leader and team members to tackle each of these ideas. In an effort to integrate leadership development into the process, they assigned many of their high-potential people as team leaders, to give them leadership experience and exposure to senior management. At a joint launch meeting the idea was emphasized that the teams were in the forefront of evolving the new strategy and structure. After developing their rapid-cycle goals and plans, the teams were off and running, reporting back to their senior champions at agreed-upon checkpoints until the final review session at the end of the hundred days.

One team, for example, focused on marketing to female investors and achieving a share gain among women in one test location. Another team set a goal to test needs-based marketing. They started with an experiment to sell a package of college-savings funds to a certain base of customers. Several other teams focused on improving the customer experience and reducing costs through ideas such as a consolidated statement and a reduction of direct mail to existing customers.

The rapid results projects provided the Retail Marketing business with a road map for improvement and change—a concrete way of translating the big vision and the tough demands into day-to-day action. It was a way to blend strategic transformation with immediate action. This blending enabled Fidelity to increase its retail market share over the subsequent two years.

Part of the challenge for rapid results leaders is to work through the tension between the need to get a result quickly and the need to push the strategic envelope. The seemingly simple change methodology used at Fidelity—similar to that employed at Public

Service of New Hampshire, GTZ, Avery Dennison, and many others described throughout this book—created a profoundly different way for the people engaged in the Fidelity retail transformation to have meaningful dialogues about rapid-cycle goals. As described in more detail in *The Boundaryless Organization*, they had new perspectives in discussing the plans for achieving those goals, what they were learning, and how it should influence the longer-term perspective.[3] And, as with those other examples, the ambitious strategic vision was not only achieved, it was sharpened and expanded as successful experience was gained.

Extraordinary and Sustainable Results

In all these cases, the objective has been to use rapid results successes to continually push out the strategic horizon that defines the visible growth opportunities for the business. In "Crafting Strategy" Henry Mintzberg wrote, "To unravel some of the confusion—and move away from the artificial complexity we have piled around the strategy-making process—we need to get back to some basic concepts. The most basic of all is the intimate connection between thought and action. That is the key to craft, and so also to the crafting of strategy."[4] As described in Chapter Six and in this chapter, the how-to of integrating thought and action in a strategic process does not have to be complex. While the way is often challenging and always unpredictable, firm logic underlies both getting started and keeping progress going. Here is the essence of the process:

1. *Define a challenging overall goal—or possibly two—for the organization, goals that cannot be achieved without significant strategic shifts.* The starting point for strategy is a set of organizational aspirations. Such goals can become the rallying point for each stage of strategic development. Developmental strategy moves continuously from planning to businesswide action. Involving as many people as possible in the initial planning phase ensures a sense of ownership on the part of the people who must get results.

2. *Within the framework of the overall goals, select four to six strategic priorities as the focus for action.* An organization can successfully act on just so much change at one time. Day-to-day business must continue. Enthusiasm for the new directions must be nurtured, and trying to do too much at once can undermine the achievement of results. No matter how important all the new directions may seem, maintain the discipline of focusing on only a few.

3. *Assign accountability for progress on each strategic priority to a senior manager to serve as champion.* For managers used to running a functional area or advancing specific tactics in a transactional environment, taking on the broader role of strategic leadership provides critical development. They must experiment with keeping the core business going while also taking responsibility for strategic progress. Bringing the champion group together on a regular basis to share responsibility for the overall business direction ensures that the strategic horizon can expand as the group explores the implications of the rapid-cycle experiences.

4. *Launch some rapid-cycle projects to generate progress and learning in a hundred days or less.* Get projects under way quickly and use the resulting experiences to refine strategic understanding. Focusing on these near-term results will not undermine long-term strategy. As we've been saying, the opposite is true. It is only by establishing rapid cycles of success and learning that a coherent strategy can emerge.

This framework is summarized in the sidebar.

> **Blending Action and Planning**
>
> 1. Define a challenging overall goal—one that requires new strategies.
> 2. Select four to six strategic priorities with the overall goal.
> 3. Assign accountability for each strategic priority.
> 4. Launch rapid results projects to generate progress and learning.

After the first round of projects, review the results and assess your portfolio of strategic priorities. As outlined in Chapter Six, you can begin to build a rhythm into the business. Strategic goals and priorities are regularly revised based on the insights gained from the action under way, and the actions that are launched are shaped by the changing strategic insights.

Strategy, integrated with action and results through the mechanism of rapid results projects, fulfills its potential as a unifying and motivational force for an organization. Since the intention is that both the planning and the action get better as experience is gained, the whole process is developmental. No matter how good it is at any moment, management is always working to make it better.

In the next chapter we explore how future leaders can mature and toughen through their participation in rapid-cycle projects and the developmental strategy process.

Key Points

- The linear approach to strategic planning keeps it in a hothouse, remote from the life of the business.

- The unintended consequence of this linear strategic planning paradigm is that actions don't follow plans— and plans are not based on urgent needs.

- Strategic planning should begin with action to address current challenges.

- Successful action yields new capacity plus fresh insights into what works in the market.

- Strategy then can evolve and sharpen as actions move forward, generating results and learning in a continuing, dynamic cycle.

11

DEVELOP LEADERS THROUGH
RESULTS ACHIEVEMENT

In the events cited thus far it is clear that when managers are asked to lead rapid-cycle, results-focused projects they almost always respond with new levels of performance. They work in new ways and elicit new responses from their people. They develop many fresh insights and innovative methods. The obvious conclusion is that success in leading groups to new heights of achievement yields important dimensions of leadership development. In this chapter we show how these successes can provide the most powerful development experiences conceivable.

Unfortunately, this phenomenon is generally ignored when companies want to improve the performance of their managers. They rarely employ a strategy to capture the learning potential of success. Instead, in true big-fix fashion, they create management development or leadership development programs as formulaic mechanisms for getting managers to improve their abilities. These activities might be classroom or off-campus workshops. They might be online training programs. They could be vigorous exercises on a mountain or jungle gym. Or they might be on-the-job activities like 360-degree feedback or annual performance reviews.

For many years, most development programs were subject-matter oriented—finance, organization dynamics, strategy, operations, human relations, information systems, communications, and so forth. These were aimed mainly at expanding the intellectual knowledge of participants. Important as it is for managers to possess

---

Richard A. Heinick and Claudio Avila Tobias provided case illustrations.

all this knowledge, these programs failed to result in significant performance outputs. Many factors contribute to this shortfall:

- Job circumstances often do not encourage or even permit the manager to apply particular learning to the job.
- Striving for performance improvement is stressful—managers may not have enough motivation to stir them to sufficiently high degrees of effort.
- Even with good motivation, managers may not know how to implement improved performance.
- If the undertaking is a very ambitious one, the managers may grow so uneasy about succeeding that they end up pouring more energy into avoidance than into achievement.

In short, innumerable obstacles stand between formal subject matter training and the useful exploitation of that training. After fifty years of ignoring this obvious dilemma, it eventually dawned on the professionals that, useful as knowledge itself might be, a leader's capacity to orchestrate major organization progress would never be developed through subject-matter expertise. People who lack this ability to make it happen simply won't produce better results than their less perspicacious counterparts no matter how brilliant their thinking.

What is this "make-it-happen" ability? It may be difficult to define, but it is not difficult to recognize when a senior leader has it. All the widely admired business leaders—from Henry Ford and Alfred Sloan to Jack Welch, Larry Bossidy, and Louis Gerstner—were able to lead their organizations through major transformations and to improve their achievements significantly, often against difficult odds.

We can also recall, with equal ease, senior people who were incapable of getting their organizations to achieve needed results even though they seemed to possess the stature and intellectual attributes of leadership. Quite frequently when their companies fail it is not because these leaders lack the knowledge of what needs doing, it is because they lack *the ability to make it happen*.

For example, a large health care organization was beginning to lose money. An extensive consulting study pointed to many inefficiencies in the organization—and clearly delineated a number of specific steps to achieve significant profitability improvement. But when senior management started to implement the recommended changes, the company's operations became chaotic, and the changes had to be terminated. This leadership group had never carried out such significant changes and simply lacked the necessary ability to do so.

The same phenomenon can frequently be seen on a smaller scale as well: a company's product lines are known to be outdated, but the organization's leaders are not capable of providing the impetus to get new products into service. Or different functions may not be collaborating as they must, but no one in leadership is capable of requiring collaboration. Also, many companies are managed by people who have consummate skill in making deals, but who, as described in Chapter Eight, seem unable to lead the ongoing organization to achieve significant performance improvements.

If there is any one capability that all leaders need to develop, it is how to mobilize the organization for change.

Solutions That Miss the Point

After awakening to the realization that subject-matter education won't develop this capability, leadership development experts also concluded that learning in a classroom can never produce these vital make-it-happen skills. If it did, the tens of thousands of graduates from fine business schools and fine company leadership development programs would possess abundant capabilities.

This realization spawned a new generation of "experiential leadership development" (or, as some prefer, "action learning") where, it is intended, leaders learn by doing. Unfortunately, even though

these programs often require some novel initiative-taking and provide stimulating experiences, we believe most of them are nonsolu-
tions because most fail to provide the one essential experience that
can make a real difference, and that is the experience of undertaking a difficult achievement challenge and carrying it out successfully.

Here is one example of the genre—an HR newsletter reporting,
with admiration, on the leadership development program of a very
large aerospace company: "This is an action learning program—i.e.,
participants learn by doing, managing team-based projects that are
targeted to address their development needs while delivering recommendations that can be implemented throughout the company."[1]

The newsletter goes on to say that in this "action learning" program, key developmental experiences include these activities:

- Exposure to key management and business issues
- Presentations of recommendations based on business case
  analysis
- Attendance at external executive development programs
- Development of personal leadership skills through highly
  focused individual analysis
- Opportunity for executive exposure, including mentorship
  arrangements

While these activities may all contribute to a leader's intellectual prowess, none of them provides opportunity for real-life learning in leading an organization to achieve challenging goals.

Joseph Raelin, in *Work-Based Learning: The New Frontier of
Management Development*, also emphasizes study-and-recommend
activities as the basis for leadership development. In *Action Learning*, David Dotlich and James Noel list twelve action elements they
consider essential, and again they are all basically intellectual
steps, with no reference to participants' achieving any sort of business results.[2] Donald Kirkpatrick, a well-known writer on leadership
development, skirts the issue in his *Evaluating Training Programs:*

"When I teach leadership, motivation, and decision making, I expect participants to understand what I teach, accept my ideas, and use them on the job. This will, of course, end up with tangible results. But how can I tell? Can I prove or even find evidence beyond a reasonable doubt that the final results occur? The answer is a resounding no. There are too many other factors that affect results."[3]

These authors, like most of the others who write about experiential or action learning for leaders, ask people to analyze, to calculate, to consider, to present, to recommend, to study, to simulate, and to reflect—all of which have value, but none of which provide experience in actually stimulating organization progress.

To teach skiing by a comparable approach, one would ask participants to study skiing, to engage in simulation exercises, and even to do papers on ski design. But *learning to ski* requires getting up on the hill and skiing, mastering the gentler slopes as a step toward mastering the more demanding ones. No matter how many ski exercises and simulations are done, only real experience on the hill—sometimes gliding, sometimes falling down—develops the skill, the know-how, and the confidence necessary for constantly improved capability.

Others Have Seen the Power

In contrast to the authors just cited, a small number do talk about the importance of real work experience in leadership development. Mark C. Maletz and Jon R. Katzenbach, in their article "Reinventing Management Development," suggest a format of one- to two-week programs separated by several months in which participants apply what they learned on the job. Henry Mintzberg, quoted in *Fast Company*, also suggests opportunities for on-the-job applications between course sessions in a much more complicated design.[4] And Morgan McCall and the other authors of *The Lessons of Experience—How Successful Executives Develop on the Job* provide many case illustrations, concluding one of the most successful with the comment, "In this case, as was true for almost all of the assignments described to us, the driving force for learning was job challenge."[5]

That finding nails the most overlooked truth in leadership development—what is true for learning to ski is true for learning to lead organizations. Rising to the challenge of achieving tough goals not only leads to better performance, it also almost always leads to the development of stronger leadership skills. These skills can serve as the foundation for even more ambitious achievements that nourish even more advanced leadership skills. The development of leaders occurs most successfully when they are required to do better. The context of striving and achieving provides the optimum learning environment.

This fundamental truth can be exploited two ways. First, leadership development can be built into whatever companies might do to achieve better performance. Second, actual performance improvement activity can be built into formal leadership development programs. The rest of the chapter elaborates on these two opportunities.

Building Development into Achievement

We noticed many years ago that the strengthening of leadership skills occurs naturally as a by-product of managerial success. That is, managers who successfully achieved breakthrough results—even fairly modest ones—seemed thereafter to have a better grasp of how to make things happen. This leadership development occurred spontaneously as a by-product of results-achieving projects without any special effort to achieve that outcome. We concluded that this accidental development can be significantly enriched by designing leadership development more deliberately into the achievement-focused projects. With some modest modifications of the project methodology, each project can become a mini–management development course.

The Avery Dennison experience described in Chapter Five was aimed at growth acceleration. During the first two years, more than a thousand rapid-cycle projects were launched around the world to achieve growth, and more than four thousand employees were actively involved. But every one of the company's growth projects aimed not only to achieve some tangible growth progress within one hundred days but also to produce some individual learning. Project leaders had to bring together diverse teams and organize them to achieve a tangible goal quickly. Every project had to be carefully planned, and teams had to consider how they could work most effectively.

Thus, in addition to more than $200 million of incremental revenue in the program's first two years, the company generated a huge amount of this kind of learning. Some of the lessons most frequently cited by participants:

- How to lead temporary teams, mixed by function and level
- How to select a growth goal achievable in a hundred days
- How to use these rapid results projects as the basis for more strategic progress
- How to involve customers and suppliers in growth projects
- How to make time available for such projects and keep their regular jobs going
- How to partner with customers in new and creative ways

Since learning was an explicit goal of the program, teams engaged in plenty of dialogue that started with the question, "What are we learning?" At the end of each round of projects, these lessons were identified and built into the next round. The significant learnings were built into the management processes of each division. In fact, the growth acceleration process became an elaborate organization development process—achieving, learning, expanding.

To have attempted to achieve such results by the more traditional logic of first developing five hundred or more team leaders around the corporation and then asking those newly developed leaders to achieve the results would have been futile. Constant successful achievement in the face of challenging odds was the greatest possible leadership learning mechanism. Bob Malchione, senior vice president of corporate technology and strategy, summarizes this outcome as follows: "Now managers begin new projects not by wondering what might go wrong but by assuming they will succeed."

And Terry Schuler, senior vice president of HR, puts it this way:

> The H1 projects give a lot of opportunity for development—for team
> leaders, for facilitators, for team members. People on H1 projects get
> a knowledge of the marketplace that they never would have gotten
> any other way. The experience of team leaders having to run an ad
> hoc team that does not report to you, where you have to work by
> influence, really is critical. Most of our managers come up within
> functions where they only have to manage people who report to
> them. But when they get to senior jobs it is a whole different game.
> Being a team leader teaches some of those necessary skills and insights.

Working the Value Chain

As the Avery Dennison experience demonstrates, managers can
develop their skills in working with customers through actual results-
focused collaboration. At a time when customer service and customer collaboration are deemed to be so important to companies,
rapid results projects provide a powerful mechanism to help people
learn how to translate slogans about customer relations into solid
customer relationships.

The example of U.S. Borax working with a large customer was
recounted in Chapter Four. Their joint rapid-cycle projects produced significant cost improvements for both companies as well as
the development of new modes of collaboration that promised
ongoing benefits thereafter. Thus, rapid results projects carried out
with customers or suppliers should be viewed as developmental
activities to enable your people to carry out even more ambitious
collaboration.

These engagements should produce some new increments of
value—cost reductions, new products, new processes, new sales.
These partnerships are outside the typical customer-supplier relationship of price negotiations, satisfaction surveys, or "customer first"
sloganeering. One ground rule in such projects is that they must
attack only goals that produce substantial and sustained gains for all

the parties involved. If there is an issue that can have only a win-lose outcome, it is a matter for negotiations, not for joint projects.

Managing such partnerships within a broader transformation process requires a company to design a methodology for involving all of the other organizations participating. Take the case of International Specialty Products (ISP), a leading specialties chemicals company in Wayne, New Jersey, which aimed at growing profits and revenue through rapid-cycle projects with customers.

ISP started with four carefully selected customers: Unilever, Colgate, Procter & Gamble, and Purdue Frederick. Management people from ISP and from each of these companies began with some dialogue aimed at identifying areas of opportunity: What might ISP be able to do that could yield major payback for the customer? Who in the customer company would be the main person to work on this opportunity? What are some possible first steps to initiate action? Conducting such interviews was new to most of the ISP people who participated and thus an important learning experience for them.

Once the customers were identified, joint teams were established to identify the most compelling projects and to pursue those projects together. For example, working with a team that included people from Colgate, ISP developed and delivered a proprietary ingredient that helped Colgate become the U.S. market leader in toothpaste. To meet the increased demand for that ingredient ISP organized some internal rapid-cycle projects that increased its manufacturing capacity 50 percent within four months. Another joint team developed an innovative solution to cut delivery costs by producing a more concentrated form of the product, saving both ISP and the customer millions of dollars in shipping and receiving costs. Other projects involved improvements in delivery time and reductions in cost through methods modifications and product spec changes.

As these initial projects quickly produced benefits all around, the basic pattern of relationships with these customers changed. As ISP's Mike Aversa, director of customer partnering, puts it, "We don't say to a customer, 'Let's work on our relationship and an outcome of that will be, some day, to increase mutual profitability.' Instead we say, 'Let's work on taking action that will produce more profitability.' We know our relationship will improve as a by-product."

More than two hundred people were involved in the initial projects with the four initial key customers. By the end of the first hundred days these people, whatever their level, had learned a huge amount about what was going on inside the customer companies, about the people in these companies, and about how to provide real value-added to them. As with the Avery Dennison customer teams, the ISP teams brought together novel mixtures of ISP people. One of its teams included a senior account manager, the corporate controller, a polymer chemist, an area production manager, the director of plant maintenance, the pharmaceutical R&D manager, and the vice president of sales. The customer's team was similarly heterogeneous.

From a strategic point of view, the successes of ISP's partnerships have prompted the company to significantly shift its marketing emphasis. Originally the company was organized around product lines; now it is organized by amount of revenue growth potential for key customers. What happened, in short, as explained in Chapter Ten, is that the rapid-cycle successes not only made ISP's growth strategy into a reality, they helped to evolve the strategy way beyond the vision that was the starting point. Working with the mixed backgrounds and skills on their teams was a profound learning experience for participants from both companies. There is no course in the world on "building customer relationships" that could have provided more powerful learning.

Results-Fueled Learning in Formal Development Programs

While the evidence is overwhelming that on-the-job development through the achievement of difficult goals is unparalleled in its effectiveness, it is not an argument for abandoning formal leadership development programs. The very same principles and learning potentials can be incorporated into formal programs. It is very similar to the idea behind so-called experiential learning, but the key difference is that the participants in the programs we advocate strive for and achieve actual, real, important company goals.

The Siemens Example

In the late 1990s, Matthias Bellmann was head of management learning at Siemens AG, a large global corporation. With some consulting collaboration, he designed into the company's development program a process for getting participants to actually achieve some tough business goals. This activity was to be launched during an initial one-week seminar and then implemented by participants back on the job, and reviewed at a second workshop four months later.

Both workshops, in addition to the results-fueled work, included conventional academic subjects, simulations, case studies, and talks by company officers. At the initial workshop participants from different businesses identified business issues that they thought might represent opportunities for them to do some creative work and contribute to corporate progress. Once they identified a menu of possible goals, participants grouped themselves into teams of four to six people, each focused on a subject that its members wanted to work on.

Each team then defined a specific, measurable goal it would commit itself to achieving in the following four months. They had to create their own road map to achieve their goal. During the four months team members would have to carry out this work while they continued their regular job responsibilities.

The ground rules called for the achievement of tangible goals such as securing an order with a new customer or reducing costs by a certain amount. Goals such as "developing a new procedure for . . . " or "recommending a new strategy to achieve . . . " were specifically barred.

The Projects

At his initial workshop, for example, Thomas Türk, a middle management participant from Sweden, said that he was certain Siemens was losing business because both in Sweden and in Norway the local

Siemens company focused almost exclusively on maximizing business within its own country. There was no good method for mobilizing regional capability to serve customer needs that crossed borders. A number of other participants who were concerned about similar issues eagerly joined together with Türk as team leader. To have a measurable goal to shoot for, the team decided to identify one potential customer operating in the two countries and to generate some new business with this customer.

This newly formed team faced all sorts of real-life challenges. First, they had to get the managers of the two country units to accept the team's self-initiated intervention. They had to identify a real company that would be the potential customer for their project. They had to create a workable plan and implement it in collaboration with the managers of both the Swedish and Norwegian Siemens companies—and do it all while each of the team members, working at a distance from one another, kept their regular jobs going. Here was a formidable set of challenges that were not easily overcome. But that was the point— the learning in this program came in tackling and mastering formidable obstacles.

The team recruited sponsors for their project in both Norway and Sweden. They decided that the greatest potentials existed in one particular industry. Within that industry they identified one customer with a large and growing operation in Sweden that could potentially be a major customer for a combined Swedish-Norwegian offering. Their "breakthrough goal"—to be achieved by the next workshop in four months—was to place some actual tenders for specific contracts with this company—tenders that represented a unified Siemens product and service offering.

And thus did each Siemens team identify a real, challenging business goal, create its own work plans and strategies, and invent the temporary groupings and mechanisms to help get its mission accomplished. Conceiving of the support needed to ensure success and then forging those alliances developed exactly the kind of leadership creativity and confidence that the program was designed to encourage. It is the kind of inventiveness and assertiveness that managers will need in the fast-moving, loosely structured organizations of the future.

When one of the initial workshops was held in Istanbul, a group of participants became interested in the challenge of expansion into Central Asia—including Uzbekistan, Kazakhstan, Turkmenistan, Iran, and Turkey. The specific goal they selected was to help some local Siemens managers succeed in making operative a fiber-optic linkage that ran through more than fifteen countries. The proof of the achievement was to be the conduct of a teleconference between Munich and Shanghai with the tie-in of a number of cities along the way.

A third team aimed at reducing certain telecommunications costs for the company. It focused on England and Germany—and set a rapid-cycle breakthrough goal of reducing costs by about 30 percent for one month a few months after getting started.

Another team got its members accepted as the catalysts for helping three Siemens companies join together to make a major sale to a large customer they all had in common. In South America, a team helped launch a new maintenance services business to augment the company's manufacturing business—and obtained the first orders for the services.

Most of the Siemens teams succeeded in their projects. The Scandinavian team succeeded in stimulating interest in both the Swedish and Norwegian companies, and they joined in responding to some tenders that might not have been available except for the collaboration. The two companies used the work with this first cross-border customer to learn how to deal with other customers.

The fiber-optic cable project succeeded, and the teleconference was held on schedule, after years of delay. The company began at once to earn revenues from the use of the line, and its reputation in the area was enhanced.

The telecommunications project developed savings worth over $1 million a year, and it set the stage for a number of similar gains following in the pattern of the team's project. Moreover, new ways to administer the telecommunications operations were designed to make sure the benefits endured.

When this program was still in its early stages, a *BusinessWeek* article reported that the company had saved about $11 million as the result of the work of thirty or forty teams.[6] By now, close to ten thousand managers have attacked real goals in the program, and the benefits are many multiples of the $11 million.

As to the learning value of such projects, let the participants speak for themselves:

- Thomas Türk on the Scandinavian project:

  We were seven members from four countries and nobody on the team had enough extra time or the "jurisdiction" to push this project through. We had to identify our strong and weak points and get a really good team sprit. Distance learning and working in virtual teams, serving customer needs across internal or external boundaries is our daily task. The project work was a small example of what we deal with daily. It was a very difficult challenge, but an easy goal would not have been so much fun to fight for. When the challenge is huge, the interest in succeeding is much higher.

- Fred Kalt, team leader of the Asian fiber-optic project:

  The fact that the goal was so difficult really focused enormous pressure and, I think, increased the motivation for the group. We achieved something others had not been able to do for a year. It made it an extremely powerful experience for us. It has given me a greater sense of confidence to deal with new business environments. I have learned a new way of entering new fields and I have learned new ways of trying to convince people that solutions are available. I urge them to look at things in new ways.

  None of us, alone, could have individually achieved this result. As a team we were able to do it.

Imagine trying to achieve these sorts of outcomes from a simulation or a case study climaxing with a presentation!

Others Have Done It Too

While Siemens is unique in terms of the scope of its programs, other companies have built results-achievement into their management development programs. The Change Acceleration Program (CAP) of GE Capital, launched in the early '90s, was one of the first programs to have groups of managers work on results-achieving projects that were designed not only to get results but also to grow managerial capability. Chase Manhattan Bank (as it was named at the time), the Morgan Bank, and AT&T all were pioneers in testing results-fueled management development programs.

The CEMEX Program

CEMEX, a $7 billion-plus global producer and marketer of cement and ready-mix concrete, employed a process very similar to the one used at Siemens. Sixty middle-to-senior managers in its International Management Program were divided into ten teams, each of which was to select a business goal to achieve.

Projects had to contribute significantly to corporate strategic priorities and provide significant learning for participants. One team developed a new concrete that enables CEMEX to generate cost savings for itself and economic benefits for real estate developers and owners. In the pilot phase the team aimed at actually making the first sale of this concrete. They succeeded and then laid out a plan for scaling up.

Another team experimented with shipping aggregates from Europe using a new mode of transportation demonstrating a workable logistics cost-reduction strategy. And another team experimented with co-branding, building products with independent producers of those products. Other rapid results projects dealt with providing additional credit to small retailers in traditional markets to enable them to expand; with getting some customers to accept product from alternative CEMEX sources, thus freeing capacity for less flexible customers; and with helping a small group of retailers learn how to sell higher-performing cements.

A number of the projects had to be modified significantly along the way because the team's initial strategies weren't working—and participants knew that a good excuse would not substitute for actual achievement. At the conclusion of the program, it was clear that the projects generated significant learning for participants and bottom-line results for the company. In addition, a number of project sponsors, impressed with what their teams accomplished, decided to adapt the rapid results strategy in their own areas of responsibility.

The program contributed to the participants' leadership mastery in a number of unique ways. They learned how to achieve results in new and unfamiliar territory, they learned how to work in virtual teams scattered across the globe, and they learned how other parts of their corporation work. At the final reporting session, an HR manager in CEMEX USA instructed the audience about logistics strategy and economics. And a Mexican IT director outlined his team's proposal for expanding high-margin sales in developing countries.

The State of Washington

In the Siemens and CEMEX examples, participants came from different parts of the company and they selected the projects they wanted to work on. The Department of Labor & Industries in the State of Washington employed a similar program, but used teams made up of actual on-the-job associates. And the teams were given direction on the subjects they were to deal with. The idea was to develop the department's managers while they worked on accelerating progress on the department's critical goals. Among other goals, projects focused on reducing workplace injuries by employees in certain industries, eliminating fraud by employers trying to avoid mandated payments, and reducing the cost of mainframe computer usage. In such programs, participants develop their ability to get things accomplished *while* actually getting things accomplished—in fact *because* they are getting things accomplished.

Although achievement is the heart of the program, certain specific learning is built into the process: how to select achievable goals; how to win acceptance by people who have not invited you into the situation; how to develop explicit work plans; how to work as a team, even when not co-located; how to modify a strategy that isn't working well enough; how to find out what groups of people are ready to do (as opposed to what their resistance may be)—and many other topics that participants feel would be useful.

These subjects can, of course, be covered in more conventional programs, but for teams committed to achieving a difficult goal, the learning is vastly different. When they hit road blocks, for example, most refuse to accept failure. Their sense of accountability impels them to find ways to overcome barriers. The conventional learning would be akin to aspiring mountain climbers in a cozy classroom discussing what they would do on Mt. Everest in a storm. Valuable as this discussion might be, only the real experience develops the real capacity.

The Chicken and the Egg in Developing Leaders

This chapter urges those responsible for developing leaders to reverse their fundamental, bedrock paradigm. That paradigm says: If you provide enough training and development to qualified people, they will be able to achieve better results. We say: When managers strive for and achieve tangible results, they will not only produce something of value for their employer, they will have an extraordinary learning experience. There is no way to duplicate this visceral experience of striving and achieving. Line managers in the pursuit of important business goals can stimulate leadership development almost every day of the year. And the same experiences can be built into formal development programs.

In this time of shrinking budgets, a development program that generates gains and profits can win strong appreciation by top management. As Matthias Bellmann says of his Siemens program, "Management development activity no longer needs to be a cost center. It can be a profit center. That is a powerful idea."

Some of the most profound learning for most participants in results-fueled learning occurs almost incidentally. They observe themselves daring to do things they never would have dared to do before. At first they assume that their participation in the program provided them the cover needed to venture into new territory. But then most get the point that no new authority was given to them. In the quest to meet their goal, they simply pushed themselves beyond old, self-imposed barriers. It dawns on them that they could do the same for themselves at any time.[7]

Key Points

- Almost every company makes huge investments to train and develop new leaders.

- If the circumstances of the participants' jobs don't encourage learning, courses can't help.

- Most so-called experiential and action learning approaches miss the point because the experiences and action are all intellectual.

- Managers develop when they are having real experiences— making things happen and learning from success.

- These results-driven experiences can be designed into formal training programs as well.

Part Four

CONCLUSION

The evidence is unmistakable. If senior leaders really wish to do so they can accelerate the progress of their organizations, probably by large increments. The concluding chapter provides some suggestions on how they can do it and how their staff functions can help.

12

CHALLENGE FOR LEADERS:

You Can Make It Happen! Will You?

The rapid results process gives people a way to get involved in the success of their company. Even the most jaundiced of people really want to be part of making their company successful. We tried many other approaches that required lots of effort and produced little in the way of results. The rapid cycle projects provide a structured way to get people to contribute and be successful. That and the time pressure—which keeps people moving ahead instead of wallowing in complex processes— are the keys to why it has worked so well for us.

—A. D. "Pete" Correll, CEO of Georgia-Pacific

So many senior executives—and I include myself in this—always want to go for the big projects that will bring in the big returns. The trouble is, many of them are so risky they very often do not pay off. And while you are spending all your time, energy, and money on those, all the short-term opportunities that might have brought you gains and created momentum are overlooked. Many senior executives have it backwards. This was a great learning experience for me as well as for everyone else here.

—Philip M. Neal, CEO of Avery Dennison

The paradigm of rapid-cycle success—using short-term results to develop implementation capacity as a key element of mastering major strategic progress—offers a huge opportunity for senior leaders. It is a practical pathway to the nimble, fast-moving organization that most managers are striving to create. But as Phil Neal notes, many senior executives have it backwards; they focus on the long-term big bets while ignoring the short-term possibilities that can ignite larger-scale transformations. So what does it take for leaders to turn this around, to capture the short-term gains, and to launch a virtuous cycle of results achievement and major capacity development?

From our experience working with hundreds of managers who have led such transformations over the past several decades, many of whom you have met in earlier chapters, capturing this opportunity does not require substantial training, a long-term executive education program, major infusions of cash, or any other kind of reformation or rewiring. On the contrary, you can move into this territory at once. All it requires is the will to get started, to experiment, and to learn along the way. In fact, if you are a senior manager and want to drive major change, you can make the same assumptions about yourself and your own role as you can about your organization, namely:

- You have the personal capacity, the hidden reserve, to get much more accomplished—more quickly—in your organization.
- Doing what you have done in the past—especially if it's been based on the big-bet paradigm—may not get you there.
- The best way to change your own leadership pattern is to get started and have some successes, rather than to analyze and prepare.
- You will learn by doing—and get better and better over time.

These assumptions suggest that if you are a CEO or senior executive wanting to drive transformation through rapid results, the best way to proceed—in fact the only way—is to get started. So if you're ready and willing to take the leap, here are the three get-started steps you need to take:

Step One: Commit publicly to some specific breakthrough results—results that are clearly a step beyond where you are now.

Step Two: Communicate your expectations about these results with demands that are clear and unambiguous.

Step Three: Provide what Pete Correll calls "a structured way to get people to contribute and be successful" and the time pressure to keep people moving ahead instead of wallowing in complex processes.

Step One: Public Commitment to Action and Results

The starting point for leading a rapid-results transformation is to take a deep breath and publicly accept personal accountability for making something important happen—no matter what the prevailing wisdom may be about what is possible, and even if you cannot see a clear path for getting there. This is the essence of transformational leadership at its most basic level. You need to have a dream about your company. This might be a full-fledged strategic vision for the coming years. Or it might be something more modest. But at least it needs to be a vision of some important ways the company needs to move or some important results it needs to achieve. You might want to do this by yourself or with some associates—but you should end up with the conviction that you have defined some major shifts that you really want to make; in fact, that you *must* make.

In almost every case of major change that we have seen or been involved in, CEOs or other senior executives have started with this commitment. It is the sand in the oyster shell, the burr under the saddle—the fuel that propels the organization into the mode of rapid change. At its most extreme level it is what *Good to Great* author Jim Collins calls a BHAG—a big, hairy, audacious goal.[1]

At the very bold end it would be equivalent to CEO Robert Galvin's commitment in the '80s to win business for Motorola in Japan by exceeding Japan's own standards of quality. At the World Bank, it was President James D. Wolfensohn's public commitment to a "world free of poverty." At GE, it was CEO Jack Welch's public determination to make GE "the most productive company on earth."

Sometimes this public commitment to major change is thrust upon a senior executive by external circumstances or crises. When Patrick O'Sullivan took over Zurich Financial's U.K. insurance company it was hemorrhaging cash. He had no choice. Similarly, when Michael D. Lockhart became chairman of flooring company Armstrong Industries, the company was operating under the cloud of pending asbestos litigation. Rather than allow the uncertainty of the asbestos albatross to sink the company, Lockhart committed to resolve the legal issues, one way or the other.

As illustrated by many of the cases in this book, if motivated by a strong desire to make something better happen, managers at almost any level of a company can start the rapid-cycle process by taking accountability for achieving some better results—fast—even if they don't know exactly how they are going to get there. It is great if the CEO takes the lead—but any department head, plant manager, or division chief can do it. You don't need to ask for permission or wait for instructions from the boss, the boss's boss, or the CEO to raise the bar. You can do it yourself and take personal responsibility for achieving some breakthrough results.

You may not be ready to make any large-scale, transformational commitment at first—nor are you required to do so. You may prefer to begin, as many do, with goals that are less ambitious—but that still break through the status quo:

- Improve performance on one dimension—such as Avery Dennison's focus on speeding growth.

- Make a modest acquisition in a short period of time, such as the successful early acquisitions by Westvaco and Meritor cited in Chapter Seven.
- Challenge one or two units to achieve a major step up in performance in months rather than years, such as Banorte's focus on ATM improvement cited in Chapter Four.
- Bring out a new product or enter a new market more quickly than ever before, as described in the Motorola radio product in Chapter Two.
- Lower costs or improve productivity quickly without reducing service or quality.

This vision must be translated into measurable goals. It's not enough to say that our company or our division will be "the best." The vision needs to have more specificity or it will just be a marketing slogan and not an impetus for change.

Two other aspects of your commitment to achievement must be explicit:

- First, it must be clear to you and to everybody else that this goal is clearly and unambiguously something well beyond what you would achieve if you didn't do something really new and different. It has to be a step up.
- Second, when you announce the goal, you have to make a personal commitment to its achievement. It is important that the goal be one on which you are willing to "bet your life."

While it should be as ambitious as you can make it, it has to be within range of achievability. But not too far within it. Making this kind of public personal commitment will be a new experience for most leadership people. When experienced managers announce new goals, they intuitively build in safety devices that provide them with escape hatches if the goals are not achieved. In this new endeavor, you need to throw away the life preserver and make a full commitment.

In other words, you should be a bit uneasy about making the public commitment to this measurable change. That is par for the course. Every leader at every level who starts a rapid-cycle transformation process goes out on a limb and takes a bit of a risk. The unequivocal commitment and the risk go hand in hand. It's a daunting prospect, especially when the pathways to getting there are not yet clear, but this is truly a case of nothing ventured, nothing gained.

Once you have the overall goal in mind (and have shared it with your people) the next step is to think about some first-step goals that can get the company moving. It should be a definition that permits you to get people to achieve some measurable results within a few months, as in the many examples in this book.

Step Two: Demand Better Results—and Make Certain Your People Produce Them

Once you publicly commit to making something happen, the game is under way. But it's not a game of solitaire, by any means. Transformation through rapid results success is a team sport and needs to involve dozens, hundreds, or even thousands of people.

Getting them involved, however, is neither an autocratic forced draft nor a polite invitation to join the game. Effective rapid results leaders need to learn how to make clear, unwavering demands on their people for more and better results, both in the short term and over the long haul. The key here is that your demands are for results—not for activities, involvement, participation, commitment, attitude adjustment, or affection. Rapid results leaders do not need to tell their people how to get something done; that is micromanaging. But they do need to make clear demands about what needs to be accomplished—specifically what results need to be achieved and by when.

For many years, we have observed that effective demand making—a key to rapid-results transformations—is an underdeveloped management skill.[2] The unequivocal demand for results, like the unequivocal goal for yourself, poses risks. Suppose you make the demand, and all the people retort, "That's impossible." Or suppose they all say they're doing their best to achieve it, then fail. Or suppose they pass the word around that you are an unreasonable manager.

Because of these risks, managers may reduce the tension by asking their people to achieve the goal *if it is possible to do so*. Or by asking the people to do the very best they can. Or by accepting backwards assignments, "Sure, boss, I'll get this done if you get Engineering to get the drawings to me." Or by committing any of the other seven deadly sins of demand making listed in the sidebar.

One of the keys to learning how to be a better demand maker is to accept the notion that most people actually benefit from being pushed, challenged, and stretched—even if they don't realize it at

---

The Seven Deadly Sins of Demand Making

1. *Back away from expectations:* "Well, OK, folks, budget for level expenses year over year, but I'd sure like to see some reductions when we get into the new year."

2. *Engage in charades:* "Look, Anne, I don't know where we're going to get a 15 percent increase in sales, but I have to put it in my budget so you've got to put it in yours."

3. *Accept see-saw trades:* "Sure, boss, we can increase sales; but you know that we'll have to give deeper discounts to do it."

4. *Set vague or distant goals:* "By this time next year I want to see a significant improvement in staff utilization in this department."

5. *Don't establish consequences:* "OK, so you screwed up. Just set goals you can reach next year."

6. *Set too many goals:* "You'll see on the screen the thirty key goals I want everyone in the division to concentrate on this year."

7. *Allow deflection to preparation and studies:* "Hey, boss, if you really want to reduce inventory, the first thing we have to do is commission a study to find out who caused the stuff to be ordered, why it is not getting used as scheduled, and whether we need to rethink our whole inventory control philosophy."

the time. There is no more powerful developmental activity for managers than the challenge of achieving tough performance goals. Morgan McCall and others from the Center for Creative Leadership uncovered this phenomenon many years ago. As cited in Chapter Eleven, when they surveyed managers, they discovered that the one developmental activity that most senior managers cite as being most key to their success was a "stretch assignment"—the challenge of doing something beyond what they had ever done before.[3] Like Henry Higgins expecting Eliza Doolittle to be a lady, if you expect your people to perform at a higher level, they often do.

Success with rapid results requires senior management's demands for better results. At Sprint Telecommunications, for example, Dave Flessas, vice president of network operations, called this the "gasp goal"—a goal so outrageous it makes people gasp in shock. He realized that only by making people gasp would he get them to break out of their long-established patterns and think differently about how to achieve ambitious goals. Flessas challenged his team to reduce the variability in how long it took to make repairs by 50 percent and at the same time reduce operating costs by $10 million per year. This goal drew gasps from his people. But then they began to make innovations they would never have considered if the goal were less challenging.

Partway into the process a team leader reported that one of their planned initiatives was not going to be feasible; therefore management should no longer count on the promised cost savings. Flessas responded by saying that the cost-savings goal was not negotiable. The team would need to find other ways of achieving it. Spurred by the unrelenting demand to achieve the cost savings, the team explored new approaches and eventually discovered even more savings than in the original initiative. At the end of a hundred days, they had achieved the goal. Equally important, spurred by Flessas's insistence on the gasp goals, they had developed their capability to adjust plans on the fly and to go after ideas aggressively and quickly. All this new capability was a valuable by-product of the pursuit of tough bottom-line goals.

As a senior leader, you can engineer a personal breakthrough by finding a business area where you sense a significant opportunity for improvement, but the people involved feel that they are already doing everything possible. In situations like this, your people will try to find an escape route. This will give you a chance to practice demand making without backing down, or rationalizing, or falling into any of the seven deadly sins of demand making. To truly transform your organization and realize your bold vision, you need to search out these situations, relish them, and practice making the demands again and again. This is the only way to learn this skill and gradually build it into your leadership repertoire.

The underlying beauty of tough demand making is that the more your people protest, the more they will actually appreciate your leadership. Yes, it sounds paradoxical—that subordinates will value you more if you make them uncomfortable. But for most people, learning comes from being pushed out of comfort zones. When people look back on high school or college experiences, they often say they learned the most from their toughest teachers. Demand making and development go hand in hand.

Step Three: Generate Learning Through Structured Experimentation and Achievement

Once you have publicly committed to a bold vision and stimulated action by demanding results, you need to create an ongoing, iterative process of achievement and learning. But this kind of process doesn't happen by itself—you have to create it, structure it, make it happen. That doesn't mean that you need to take over the achievement of goals from your people, but it does mean that you have to be involved and get your hands dirty. Virtually all the cases cited throughout the book began tentatively, experimentally. Senior managers who wanted to accelerate the pace of progress carved off some initial projects to see what they could learn from the experience.

The actions that they took—Avery Dennison, Georgia-Pacific, Zurich U.K., Westvaco—were neither prescribed nor formulaic.

They were experimental, and the processes that these companies launched focused equally on learning and on achievement. In fact, one of the most important messages that must be conveyed in launching the process is that the rapid results projects are truly skunkworks—protected experiments. Nobody should be penalized for not fully achieving the goal, as long as they generate learning about how to get to the goal in other ways. Thus part of the structure that rapid results leaders create is a safe space where people can experiment and try new things, even if they don't always work quite as expected. Of course, this doesn't mean that people can just fake it with a good old college try. Part of the magic for rapid results leaders is to work through this tension with their people—the need to get a result quickly while pushing the envelope with ideas that may or may not bear fruit.

Working through this tension means that the simple structures that senior managers set up to launch rapid results experiments must provide mechanisms for senior people to stay engaged in the change process—to have meaningful dialogues about the breakthrough goals, about the plans for achieving those goals, and about progress, learning, and obstacles along the way. Empowering people and giving them room to roam and learn doesn't mean leaving them alone to fend for themselves in the wilderness. In our experience, effective change leaders create opportunities—through an organized structure—to stay engaged. Nobody else but you, the senior executive, can create that structure—just as nobody else can articulate the bold vision and make the clear demands. This doesn't mean that you need to be a day-to-day part of the team, but you certainly need to be engaged with the team during the ride.

Behind Every Great Leader . . . Is a Great Staff

While engaged in this high-wire juggling act, senior leaders need to have key staff support functions that can help the business move forward, without complicating the dilemmas or overly weighing them down on one side or the other of the short-term versus long-

term dilemma. To do this, the heads of staff functions—chief financial officers, chief information officers, HR officers, and others—also
need to play different roles. Instead of thinking of themselves as
delivering professional expertise and tools that line managers will
eventually use to get results, they need to think of themselves as
equally accountable for delivering business results.

For most leaders of staff functions and their people, this is a
huge shift. Most of their training and experience focuses on technical skills. IT people learn programming, database architecture,
data center configurations, and the like; Finance staff focus on balance sheet management, cash flow, and financial analysis; HR specialists develop expertise in training, performance management,
compensation planning, and so forth. Nowhere in the résumé is
a course or a program, or even a requirement, to produce business
results. That is usually considered to be the line general manager's
purview. Thus, staff people usually spend most of their time developing programs, tools, systems, controls, or other units of "expert
input" that they offer up to line managers who, they assume, will
then use them to get results.

Line managers often feel that these technical inputs from staff
experts are overly academic—and don't provide the help they really
need. Programs take too long, or cost too much, or don't provide
benefits that will really make a difference. Comments like "they just
don't get it" or "it's elegant, but it will never get us more sales in
Europe" are commonplace.

On the other hand, staff people often feel that line managers
don't appreciate the power of the staff contributions or they just
can't implement their programs in the right way. Staff professionals
often say things like "What we gave them was the right tool, but
they just couldn't implement it," or "Those managers don't understand what it takes to get the results they are asking for."

This recurring tension between line and staff managers needs to
be eliminated for an organization to continuously renew itself and
succeed at transformation. Line and staff managers need to engage
in a partnership where both sides feel accountable for achieving

results *and* building the ongoing organizational capacity to change. As senior executives articulate the bold vision and sharpen the demand for results, they need staff specialists to be with them every step of the way, not just whispering in their ears but out on the playing field taking joint responsibility for making it happen. When line and staff executives work together effectively in the context of a shared rapid results framework, it can be a powerful combination.

For example, when Lawrence J. Toole was GE Capital's senior vice president for HR, he insisted that the HR staff assume some account-ability for the successful integration of GE Capital's many acquisitions. Since making acquisitions was a key plank in GE Capital's growth strat-egy, Toole was convinced that HR could take the lead in making the acquisition process itself a core capability of the company. He assigned Lawrence J. DeMonaco to lead a company-wide effort to capture the best practices developed in the company's past integrations. Working with managers who had been on both sides of previous acquisitions, DeMonaco created the GE Capital model, since documented in a *Har-vard Business Review* article.[4] This model allowed GE Capital to success-fully integrate an average of fifty new companies per year for several years and to become one of the largest and most profitable financial services companies in the world.

As this example illustrates, it is not only the line executives who can focus simultaneously on both the long term and short term. Toole realized that each acquisition needed to produce short-term results, but he created a framework for using the short-term results as a way of strengthening basic capacity and fostering a longer-term growth strategy. He didn't wait for CEO Gary Wendt or any other line executive to make these connections. He took the lead and created a partnership with general managers to make it happen.

For staff executives to be effective in a rapid results context, they need to take this kind of initiative—to get on the field and not wait for an invitation to come out of the stands. This doesn't mean that you, as a staff executive, will always be successful. But it is important to try.

For example, Ford Calhoun, the chief information officer of Glaxo-SmithKline Pharmaceuticals, proposed that no business applications development project be approved unless it could pay for itself in twelve months or less. He was discouraged from proceeding. This was too big a change for the line organization. It would also mean that the IT community would have to shape projects completely differently. Undeterred, Calhoun worked with his own management team and their IT people to start carving up projects so that they would have shorter-term payoffs. He began to demonstrate the value of the approach. Eventually he convinced the senior executive team to make this a policy. The results were dramatic—with business applications projects producing returns on investments at more than double their historic rates.

Another aspect of this approach, as many examples throughout the book—including Toole and Calhoun—illustrate, is that staff not only takes accountability and initiative, but actually collaborates actively with line management. The job of staff, in this respect, is not just to produce recommendations, systems, reports, papers, or controls. It is to join in with others to make things happen.

Patrick O'Sullivan provides another good example. After he completed the turnaround of Zurich Financial Services' U.K. general insurance unit as its CEO, as detailed in Chapters Five and Six, he became group finance director for Zurich worldwide, with a mandate to make major improvements in the financial management of the company. Previously, Finance had played a traditional staff role. For example, its people had been analyzing the need for better cash management for some time but had taken no decisive action.

Within three weeks of starting in his new role, O'Sullivan and the top Finance leaders from around the world developed a cash management action plan. Then, in a Work-Out session including both Operations managers and Finance people, a set of actions was agreed upon. In less than three months, an additional $1 billion in internal cash was freed up within the company—worth millions in bottom-line savings and additional income opportunities. Additional Finance staff efforts using Work-Out or rapid results teams drove tens of millions of dollars to the company's bottom line and helped to strengthen the regular financial reporting.

Staff leaders who take this kind of high-impact approach—who accept accountability, take initiative, and get involved in the real work—have a tremendous opportunity to make a difference, both in the short term and over time. Yes, it takes courage, the willingness to break out of established patterns, and the willingness to deal with people who think that staffs should remain in the background. But when senior executive leaders and their staff functional leaders gain true alignment around rapid results and the simultaneous development of capacity, they can create organizations and institutions that will stand the test of time.

Blending Short-Term Focus with Long-Term Focus

As rapid results leaders convey bold visions, make demands, and create a structure for experimentation and learning, they also progress on clarifying their own long-term vision and the short-term results that must be achieved. This bifocal perspective is essential for effecting a rapid results transformation. As emphasized earlier, in the context of bold, longer-term vision, rapid results projects build momentum, provide learning, and create capacity. At the same time, the longer-term vision needs to be constantly sharpened, tested, and updated through iterative rapid results. Transforming an organization is never a straight line; rather it is a process of successive approximation.

Learning to be comfortable with this bifocal perspective—without getting blurred vision—is one of the major challenges that most leaders face. Pressures abound to focus on one side or the other of the equation—from Wall Street, the board, customers, the media, and employees. And often these pressures shift from one day to the next. The challenge, of course, is to keep focused on both sides—and to maintain the umbilical cord of learning between them.

When William J. McDonough was president of the Federal Reserve Bank of New York, the lead bank in the Federal Reserve System, he realized that changes in the global monetary system required the New York "Fed" to reshape a number of long-standing ways of doing business. He assembled a small team to manage a process of "strategic dialogue" for himself and the senior team. While this strategic thinking process was going on, McDonough simultaneously encouraged a number of these same senior executives to test some of the emerging ideas through a series of rapid results projects.

For example, one team decreased the cycle time for responding to short-term foreign exchange requests from international central banks. Another team reduced by 50 percent the time required to assemble some key data it published to support the Federal Reserve's Open Market Committee.[5] Both of these rapid results projects, and others, not only provided short-term results for the bank but also developed the capacity of the entire bank to carry out the more ambitious changes of the longer-term strategy.

Had McDonough focused only on long-term strategic shifts, his organization would likely not have had the capacity to carry them out. In fact, in preceding years many "big strategies" had been promulgated with very little implementation progress. Working both the short-term and long-term perspectives simultaneously was key to McDonough's success at keeping the New York Federal Reserve Bank at the center of major economic and financial system change.

The challenge for all the McDonoughs of the world who are serious about major change is to manage the bifurcation between short-term and long-term focus. It is easy to get trapped on one side or the other of the great divide. As described earlier in the book, much of the prevailing wisdom in the management literature suggests that short-term focus is bad, that it takes away from creating a sustainable enterprise that might need to sacrifice immediate gains for the long-term good. Yet investors, managers, and our basic human nature want immediate gratification. Without short-term results, the organization may never develop the capacity to reach the long-term goals

As emphasized earlier, leaders who are effective in driving change through rapid results can blend the bold long-term perspective with shorter-cycle activities. This management approach gives leaders the tools to manage a complex portfolio of rapid results initiatives along with longer-term, large-scale changes—all in the context of an evolving vision and strategy for the business.

No Need to Wait

Producing rapid results while building long-term capacity for change, in the context of longer-term visions and strategies, is the challenge we have laid out for executives in this book. But it is a challenge that does not require a cosmic shift to make sure that the stars and moon—or line and staff—are properly aligned. You can start now, whether you are in a staff or line position, with whatever challenges are at hand.

The message that we have emphasized throughout this book is that the best way to develop the capacity for large-scale, long-term change is to get started with short-term results. Now. Organizations across the world are being challenged on many fronts in this ever-changing global environment. Encouraging and driving rapid results will give your organization greater capacity to survive and thrive in the midst of these whitewater rapids. The starting point is you. Will you do it? If not, who will?

Key Points

- Senior executives can take the lead in driving rapid results and the development of their organization's capability for continual change.

- The best way to lead rapid results is to plunge right in and learn by doing:

  Publicly commit to making something important happen.

  Select one or two improvements or changes you really want to make.

  Demand better results in those areas and hold people accountable for them.

  Encourage experimentation and learning.

  Set up a structure to drive results and get personally engaged in it.

  Do it once—then again and again.

- Balance long-term visions and planning with the short-term achievement of results.

- The heads of staff functions can also provide leadership for rapid results and change capability—and can partner with line executives to create ongoing success.

- Get started now.

Notes

Preface

1. *Property-Casualty Insurance Annual*, 1994, McKinsey & Company.
2. Bibliography, an annotated list of publications by RHS&A, also available at www.RHSA.com.

Chapter 1

1. Thomas J. Peters and Robert H. Waterman Jr., *In Search of Excellence* (New York: Warner Books, 1982).
2. Jim Collins, *Good to Great* (New York: HarperCollins, 2001).
3. Jack Welch with John A. Byrne, *Jack: Straight from the Gut* (New York: Warner Business Books, 2001); Larry Bossidy and Ram Charan, *Execution: The Discipline of Getting Things Done* (New York: Crown Business, 2002); Andrew S. Grove, *Only the Paranoid Survive: How to Identify and Exploit the Crisis Points That Challenge Every Business* (New York: Random House, 1996); Albert J. Dunlap with Bob Andelman, *Mean Business: How I Save Bad Companies and Make Good Companies Great* (New York: Simon & Schuster, 1996).
4. John P. Kotter, *Leading Change* (Boston: Harvard Business School Press), 1996, p. 21; John P. Kotter and Dan S. Cohen, *The Heart of Change: Real-Life Stories of How People Change Their Organizations* (Boston: Harvard Business School Press, 2002); and John P. Kotter, "Leading Change: Why Transformation

Efforts Fail," *Harvard Business Review*, March-April 1995, pp. 59–67.

5. Michael Beer, Russell Eisenstat, and Bert Spector, *The Critical Path to Corporate Renewal* (Boston: Harvard Business School Press, 1990).

6. Robert G. Eccles, Nitin Nohria, and James D. Berkeley, *Beyond the Hype: Rediscovering the Essence of Management* (Boston: Harvard Business School Press, 1992); Ronald N. Ashkenas, "Beyond the Fads: How Leaders Drive Change with Results," in *Managing Strategic and Cultural Change in Organizations*, edited by Craig Eric Schneier (New York: Human Resource Planning Society, 1995).

7. Nadim Matta and Ron Ashkenas, "Why Good Projects Fail Anyway," *Harvard Business Review*, September 2003, pp. 109–116.

8. Gary Hamel and Liisa Välikangas, "The Quest for Resilience," *Harvard Business Review*, September 2003, pp. 52–63.

Chapter 2

1. From the Apollo-13 Web site: http://science.ksc.nasa.gov/history/apollo/apollo-13/apollo-13.html. Access date February 8, 2005.

2. Robert H. Schaffer, "Managers Can Avoid Wasting Time," Program II: Harvard Business Review Video Series (Deerfield, IL: MTI Film & Video, 1985).

3. Robert H. Schaffer, *High-Impact Consulting: How Clients and Consultants Can Work Together to Achieve Extraordinary Results* (San Francisco: Jossey-Bass, 2002).

Chapter 3

1. Andrew S. Grove, *Only the Paranoid Survive: How to Identify and Exploit the Crisis Points That Challenge Every Business* (New York: Random House, 1996).

Chapter 4

1. Michael Hammer, "Deep Change: How Operational Innovation Can Transform Your Company," *Harvard Business Review,* April 2004, pp. 85–93.
2. Robert Hayes, Gary Pisano, David Upton, and Steven Wheelwright, *Operations, Strategy and Technology: Pursuing the Competitive Edge* (New York: Wiley, 2004).
3. *2002 OSH Summary Estimates Chart Package.* December 18, 2003. Available online: http://www.bls.gov/iif/oshwc/osh/os/ osch0026.pdf. Access date February 9, 2005.
4. Suzanne C. Francis and Matthew K. McCreight, "Restoring Health to Workers Compensation," *Bureaucrat,* Spring 1990, *19,* no. 1, pp. 12–15.
5. Robert A. Neiman, *Execution Plain and Simple: Twelve Steps to Achieving Any Goal on Time and on Budget* (New York: McGraw-Hill, 2004).

Chapter 5

1. Merhdad Baghai, Stephen Coley, and David White, *The Alchemy of Growth: Practical Insights for Building the Enduring Enterprise* (London: Perseus, 1990).
2. Avery Dennison Annual Report, 2003, p. 4.
3. David Ulrich, Steve Kerr, and Ron Ashkenas, *The GE Work-Out: How to Implement GE's Revolutionary Method for Busting Bureaucracy and Attacking Organizational Problems—Fast!* (New York: McGraw-Hill, 2002).

Chapter 6

1. Michael Beer, R. A. Eisenstat, and Bert Spector, "Why Change Programs Don't Produce Change," *Harvard Business Review,* November-December 1990, pp. 158–166.

Chapter 8

1. David Henry, "Mergers: Why Most Big Deals Don't Pay Off," *BusinessWeek*, October 14, 2002, pp. 60–70; Larry Selden and Geoffrey Colvin, "M&A Needn't Be a Loser's Game," *Harvard Business Review*, June 2003, pp. 70–79.
2. Ronald N. Ashkenas and Suzanne C. Francis, "Integration Managers: Special Leaders for Special Times," *Harvard Business Review*, November-December 2000, pp. 108–116.
3. "Company News: Westvaco and Mead to Merge in a $3 Billion Deal," *New York Times*, August 30, 2001, Late Edition Final, p. C-5.

Chapter 9

1. For a fuller treatment of this case study, see Nadim Matta and Ron Ashkenas, "Why Good Projects Fail Anyway," *Harvard Business Review*, September 2003, pp. 109–116.
2. This and other quotes from Noël Pallais are excerpted from an interview conducted by Ronnie Hammad of the World Bank in December 2002 as part of a program by the World Bank's Africa Region to debrief clients who are playing a key role in pioneering development work.
3. This incident was relayed to the author by Johannes Malaki, June 2004.
4. Excerpted from an e-mail message from Donald Bundy, lead specialist, school health and nutrition, at the World Bank.

Chapter 10

1. Henry Mintzberg, "Crafting Strategy," *Harvard Business Review*, July-August 1987, pp. 66–75; quote on p. 66.
2. Gary Hamel and Liisa Välikangas, "The Quest for Resilience," *Harvard Business Review*, September 2003, pp. 52–65.

3. Ron Ashkenas, Dave Ulrich, Todd Jick, and Steve Kerr, *The Boundaryless Organization: Breaking the Chains of Organizational Structure* (San Francisco: Jossey-Bass, 2002), pp. 118–119.
4. Mintzberg, 1987, p. 68.

Chapter 11

1. Louis Carter, editor, "Case Study: Boeing," *Link & Learn Newsletter*, Burlington, MA: Linkage Press, 2001.
2. Joseph Raelin, *Work-Based Learning: The New Frontier of Management Development* (Upper Saddle River, NJ: Prentice Hall, 2000); David Dotlich and James Noel, *Action Learning: How the World's Top Companies Are Re-Creating Their Leaders and Themselves* (San Francisco: Jossey-Bass, 1998).
3. Donald Kirkpatrick, *Evaluating Training Programs: The Four Levels* (2nd edition) (San Francisco: Berrett-Koehler, 1998), p. 65.
4. Mark C. Maletz and Jon R. Katzenbach, "Reinventing Management Development," *Leader to Leader*, 13, Summer 1999, pp. 47–52; Jennifer Reingold, "You Can't Create a Leader in a Classroom," *Fast Company*, 40, November 2000, pp. 286–294.
5. Morgan W. McCall Jr., Michael M. Lombardo, and Ann M. Morrison, *The Lessons of Experience: How Successful Executives Develop on the Job* (New York: Lexington Books, 1988), p. 15.
6. Jack Ewing (Frankfurt), "Siemens: Building a 'B-School' In Its Own Back Yard," *BusinessWeek*, November 15, 1999, pp. 281–282.
7. Matthias Bellmann and Robert Schaffer, "Freeing Managers to Innovate," *Harvard Business Review*, June 2001, pp. 32–33.

Chapter 12

1. James Collins, *Good to Great* (New York: HarperCollins, 2001).
2. Robert H. Schaffer, "Demand Better Results—And Get Them," *Harvard Business Review*, March-April 1991, pp. 142–149.

3. Morgan W. McCall Jr., Michael M. Lombardo, and Ann M. Morrison, *The Lessons of Experience: How Successful Executives Develop on the Job* (New York: Lexington Books, 1988).
4. Ronald N. Ashkenas, Lawrence J. DeMonaco, and Suzanne C. Francis, "Making the Deal Real: How GE Capital Integrates Acquisitions," *Harvard Business Review*, January 1998, pp. 165–178.
5. Nadim Matta and Sandy Krieger, "From IT Solutions to Business Results," *Business Horizons*, 44, no. 6, November-December 2001, pp. 45–50.

Acknowledgments

Our greatest debt of gratitude is to the business and social leaders whose creative and determined use of a rapid results approach enabled them to achieve the outstanding results chronicled in this book. Putting your chips on this methodology is to some extent an act of bravery. The leaders who do so have to venture outside the conventional "let's do a study and have a program" mode of accelerating organization progress. They must symbolically stand up, define a clear goal, and communicate, "I am committed to achieve this goal. I don't have any 'explanations' tucked away in my pocket that I can pull out in case of failure. So I guess I have no alternative but to achieve it."

The collaborative nature of the authorship of the book is expressed by the author credits for each chapter. Case material was provided by our associates Catherine V. Beavan, Richard A. Heinick, Elaine M. Mandrish, Catherine Paul-Chowdhury, Rudi A. Siddik, and Claudio Avila Tobias. One case was contributed by Thomas Leder of HLP-Organizational Consultants, our Frankfurt-based affiliate. In addition, our associates Patrice Murphy, Katherine Liu, Wes Siegal, and Justin Wasserman provided a variety of important backup support.

As described in the Preface, the rapid results methodology has been developed and tested over many years by the principals of Robert H. Schaffer & Associates. The authors would like to acknowledge the contributions made to this evolution by a number of our former associates, in particular Richard A. Bobbe.

Edith Goldenhar read the manuscript and provided some valuable editing suggestions.

Amy Beebe, Emilieanne Koehnlein, and Federico Lara provided major help with typography, manuscript preparation, and research. Maura Pratt and Joanne Young provided invaluable logistical and administrative support and coordination.

The Authors

Robert H. Schaffer (rhs@rhsa.com) founded Robert H. Schaffer & Associates and continues as a senior partner of the firm. RHS&A helps impatient managers accelerate the pace of change and achieve major performance improvements using the methods described in this book. The firm has worked with Johnson & Johnson, JP Morgan-Chase, Fidelity Investments, General Electric, General Reinsurance, IBM, Avery Dennison, Siemens AG, the World Bank, and many other companies and government and social agencies around the world.

Schaffer earned an undergraduate degree in engineering and a doctorate in management and psychology from Columbia University. He helped found the journal *Consulting to Management*, and has been an editor there for many years. He has written two previous books—*The Breakthrough Strategy* (HarperBusiness, 1988) and *High-Impact Consulting* (Jossey-Bass, 2002)—and has published about sixty articles.

Ronald N. Ashkenas (ron@rhsa.com) is a managing partner at RHS&A. He is an internationally recognized consultant, executive coach, and speaker on organizational transformation. He was one of the lead consultants for General Electric's "Work-Out" process and helped to develop GE Capital's approach to acquisition integration. He is the coauthor of three previous books: *The Boundaryless Organization* (2nd edition, Jossey-Bass 2002), *The Boundaryless Organization Field Guide* (Jossey-Bass, 1999), and *The GE Work-Out* (McGraw-Hill, 2002). Four of his articles have appeared in the *Harvard Business*

Review. Ashkenas earned an undergraduate degree from Wesleyan University, a master's in education from Harvard, and a doctorate in organizational behavior from Case Western Reserve University.

Each of the six chapter coauthors has worked with Schaffer and Ashkenas at RHS&A for fifteen or more years, practicing and developing the methodologies described in this book. Each of them provided important consulting support to many of the cases described in *Rapid Results!*

Suzanne C. Francis (scf@rhsa.com) served as a managing partner of the firm from 1997 to 2005 and is currently a senior partner. For a number of years she has devoted major attention to the challenge of making mergers and acquisitions succeed, and she leads the firm's work in that area. She has written a number of articles on this topic, including two landmark pieces in the *Harvard Business Review.* Before joining RHS&A Francis worked for Xerox Corporation as well as for a number of public and nonprofit organizations. She holds a master's degree in business from the Yale School of Management.

Matthew K. McCreight (mkm@rhsa.com) is a managing partner of the firm and leads the firm's Work-Out practice. He has helped many large corporations in Europe and North America carry out highly successful global transformations, financial turnarounds, and mergers; he has helped major government agencies and health care and nonprofit organizations apply the rapid results focus to improve performance. He is the author of a number of articles on rapid results and major organizational transformation. He holds a master's degree in management from Yale School of Management and an undergraduate degree in economics from Wesleyan University.

Nadim F. Matta (nfm@rhsa.com) is a member of the firm's Management Committee and leads the firm's rapid results practice in developing countries. He has collaborated with the World Bank and other aid agencies to introduce the rapid results approach in Latin America, Africa, and South Asia and to train local consultants to expand the process. He also has led a number of large-scale corporate change efforts in the United States. Early in his career, Matta worked at the U.S. Agency for International Development and Save the Children to manage relief and rehabilitation efforts in Lebanon during the country's civil war. He has written a number of articles on the subjects of rapid results, implementation capacity, and project management, including one in the *Harvard Business Review*. He holds an undergraduate degree from MIT and master's degrees from the Yale School of Management and the American University of Beirut.

Keith E. Michaelson (kem@rhsa.com) is a member of the firm's Management Committee and leads the firm's work in training internal consultants in rapid results. He has applied the rapid results approach to a number of public utilities and financial services organizations. For the past several years he has focused much of his professional attention on helping managers understand the linkage between strategy and implementation, and he has written a number of articles on this subject. Michaelson received his undergraduate degree from Brown University and a master's in business from the Yale School of Management.

Robert A. Neiman (ran@rhsa.com) is an emeritus partner. He joined the firm in its earliest days and was a member of the Management Committee for most of his career. He has led significant performance and strategic improvement efforts in industry, education, health care, and government as well as contributing to the development of the firm's practice. He is the author of *Execution Plain and Simple*, published by McGraw-Hill in 2004, and numerous articles. He holds an engineering degree and a master's in business administration from the Harvard Business School.

Harvey A. Thomson (hat@rhsa.com) heads the firm's Canadian office. He has worked across the spectrum of RHS&A practice areas, and has also specialized in bringing a results focus and discipline to the so-called softer performance areas such as employee health, workplace safety, leadership diversity, and flexible working arrangements. Prior to joining RHS&A, Thomson was an assistant professor in the McGill University School of Management. He has written a number of articles on results-driven performance improvement, including one in the *Harvard Business Review*. He holds a doctorate in organizational behavior from Case Western Reserve University.

The authors can be reached at

30 Oak Street
Stamford, Connecticut 06905–5313
phone: 203-322-1604
e-mail: info@rhsa.com
Web site: www.rhsa.com

Index